40 Short

NORTH YORKSHIRE

Produced by AA Publishing
© AA Media Limited 2011

Researched and written by
Jon Sparks

Additional material and walks by
David Winpenny (updated by Jon Sparks
and David Winpenny)

Commissioning Editor: David Popey
Series Management: Sandy Draper
Series Design: Tracey Butler
Copy-editor: Ann F Stonehouse
Proofreader: Pam Stagg
Picture Researcher: Liz Allen
Internal Repro and Image Manipulation:
Sarah Montgomery
Cartography provided by the Mapping
Services Department of AA Publishing
Production: Lorraine Taylor

Published by AA Publishing (a trading name
of AA Media Limited, whose registered office
is Fanum House, Basing View, Basingstoke,
Hampshire RG21 4EA; registered number
06112600)

 This product
includes mapping
data licensed from the Ordnance Survey®
with the permission of the Controller of
Her Majesty's Stationery Office. © Crown
Copyright 2011. All rights reserved.
Licence number 100021153.

A04616

978-0-7495-6906-8
978-0-7495-6918-1 (SS)

Colour separation by AA Digital

Printed by Oriental Press

Visit AA Publishing at theAA.com/sh

A CIP catalogue record for this book is
available from the British Library.

The contents of this book are believed
correct at the time of printing. Nevertheless,
the publishers cannot be held responsible
for any errors or omissions or for changes
in the details given in this book or for
the consequences of any reliance on the
information it provides. This does not affect
your statutory rights. We have tried to
ensure accuracy in this book, but things do
change and we would be grateful if readers
would advise us of any inaccuracies they
may encounter.

We have taken all reasonable steps to ensure
that these walks are safe and achievable
by walkers with a realistic level of fitness.
However, all outdoor activities involve a
degree of risk and the publishers accept
no responsibility for any injuries caused to
readers whilst following these walks. For
more advice on walking safely see page 144.
The mileage range shown on the front cover
is for guidance only – some walks may be
less than or exceed these distances.

Some of the walks may appear in other AA
books and publications.

Picture credits

The Automobile Association would like
to thank the following photographers,
companies and picture libraries for their
assistance in the preparation of this book.

1 AA/T Mackie; 6 AA/M Kipling; 10 AA/D
Clapp; 17 AA/D Clapp; 28 AA/M Kipling; 38
AA/P Bennett; 44 AA; 54 AA/M Kipling; 64
AA/M Kipling; 74/5 AA/M Kipling; 94 © Mark
Sutherland/Alamy; 107 AA/T Mackie; 117
AA/T Mackie; 136/7 AA/T Mackie.

Every effort has been made to trace the

Opposit

40 Short Walks in

NORTH YORKSHIRE

Contents

Rating
Each walk is rated for its relative difficulty compared to the other walks in this book. Walks marked ✚ are likely to be shorter and easier with little total ascent. The hardest walks are marked ✚✚✚

Walking in Safety
For advice and safety tips see page 144.

Introduction

North Yorkshire is big. It is, by a clear margin, England's largest county. And it is beautiful, too. The county claims the lion's share of two national parks, the Yorkshire Dales and North York Moors – a distinction no other county can match. Add in two Areas of Outstanding Natural Beauty (Nidderdale and the Howardian Hills), and nearly half of the county is officially designated as landscape of the highest quality. And much of the rest – as many of these walks demonstrate – is also gorgeous.

North Yorkshire's landscape is dominated by two main blocks of upland, with the Yorkshire Dales rising in the west and the North York Moors in the north-east. Between them is a broad swathe of rich agricultural lowland, known as the Vale of Mowbray in the north and the Vale of York in the south.

Upland Areas

The Yorkshire Dales National Park, with the adjoining Nidderdale AONB, forms the core of the most extensive upland area. Here are found peaks which can properly be called mountains. The most famous and charismatic of these are the 'Three Peaks': Pen-y-Ghent, Ingleborough and Whernside. At 2,414ft (736m), Whernside is the highest peak in the county.

Climbing the peaks is beyond the scope of this book, but they provide a fabulous backdrop to many of the walks. Walk 38, for example, is right in the middle of the Three Peaks. It also takes a close look at the iconic Ribblehead viaduct, one of the grandest monuments of the great age of railway building.

There's plenty more drama in the Dales, with crags, gorges and waterfalls. This is also classic limestone country, where streams disappear into dark potholes or surge out of mysterious caves. Several walks pass close to such features, and Walk 40 even gives you the chance of a short, safe venture into the underground world.

Moorland

The North York Moors, as the name suggests, is an area of moorland rather than mountains, a place of wide horizons. There's drama where the land rears up from the lowlands in the west, and again along the wave-fretted coast. The moors form the largest area of heather moorland in England. In full bloom, this is among the greatest natural displays of colour to be seen anywhere in the world.

To the south of the moors lies the green sweep of Ryedale, also known as the Vale of Pickering. Then the land rises again to the Howardian Hills and the

Opposite: The Hole of Horcum

Yorkshire Wolds. The northernmost of the chalk ridges of England, the Wolds are a spacious land of rolling skylines and deep-cut, often dry, valleys.

North Yorkshire has been inhabited for millennia, and many of the walks reveal aspects of its long, complex and intriguing history. York is one of England's greatest historic cities, and of course there is a walk here to explore it. Elsewhere, North Yorkshire is still a largely rural county, dotted with comfortable market towns like Thirsk and Richmond, and many lovely villages. Walks also visit the historic spa of Harrogate and the famous port of Whitby. Another route strides along the cliffs into Scarborough, Britain's first seaside resort.

North Yorkshire is not just big, not just beautiful, but rich and diverse and full of surprises. While these walks can hardly reveal everything it has to offer, there's no better way to begin your exploration.

Using the Book

This collection of 40 walks is easy to use. Use the locator map to select your walk, then turn to the map and directions of your choice. The route of each walk is shown on a map and clear directions help you follow the walk. Each route is accompanied by background information about the walk and area.

INFORMATION PANELS

An information panel for each walk details the total distance, landscape, paths, parking, public toilets and any special conditions that apply, such as restricted access or level of dog friendliness. The minimum time suggested for the walk is for reasonably fit walkers and doesn't allow for stops.

ASCENT AND DIFFICULTY

An indication of the gradients you will encounter is shown by the rating ▲▲▲ (no steep slopes) to ▲▲▲ (several very steep slopes). Walks are also rated for difficulty. Walks marked ✚✚✚ are likely to be shorter and easier with little total ascent. The hardest walks are marked ✚✚✚.

MAPS AND START POINTS

There are 40 maps covering the walks. Some walks have a suggested option in the same area. Each walk has a suggested Ordnance Survey map. The start of each walk is given as a six-figure grid reference prefixed by two letters indicating which 100km square of the National Grid it refers to. You'll find more information on grid references on most Ordnance Survey maps.

CAR PARKING

Many of the car parks suggested are public, but occasionally you may find you have to park on the roadside or in a lay-by. Please be considerate when you leave your car, ensuring that access roads or gates are not blocked and that other vehicles can pass safely.

DOGS

We have tried to give dog owners useful advice about how dog friendly each walk is. Please respect other countryside users. Keep your dog under control, especially around livestock, and obey local bylaws and other dog control notices. Remember, it is against the law to let your dog foul in public areas, especially in villages and towns.

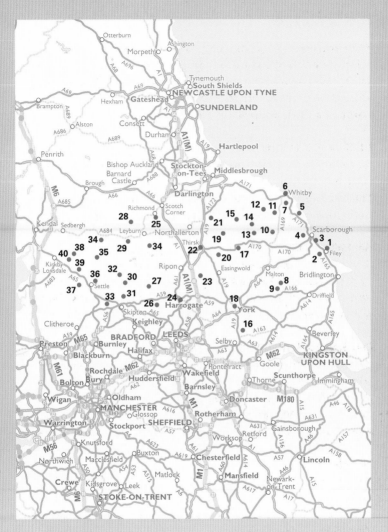

KEY TO WALKING MAPS

---→---	Walk Route		Built-up Area
❶	Route Waypoint		Woodland Area
----	Adjoining Path	🚻	Toilet
☼	Viewpoint	🅿	Car Park
•	Place of Interest	⊞	Picnic Area
⌂	Steep Section	)(	Bridge

CRUMBLING CLIFFS AT FILEY

An easy walk over a dramatic headland and the beach that shelters behind it.

You don't need to be an expert geologist to see the contrast between the ragged headland of Filey Brigg and Bempton Cliff across the bay. Filey Brigg's crumbling red cliffs look like badlands from the Wild West, while Bempton Cliff is vertical and greyish-white. Bempton Cliff is chalk, in fact the northernmost chalk cliff in Britain.

The cliffs of Carr Naze, especially on the side facing the bay, are mostly composed of glacial deposits or till, which are soft and easily eroded. Underlying these, and showing more clearly on the seaward side, are a succession of limestone and sandstone strata. At low tide these rocks can be seen to form an extensive platform on the bay side and towards Brigg End. When the tide is low it is possible to cross the platform linking the end of Carr Naze to the sandy beach, but the rocks are slippery and the paths on the flank of Carr Naze are steep and eroded. Try it if you like, but at your own risk.

From Roman Camp to Holiday Camp

Crumbling they may be, but the cliffs have sheltered Filey Bay for millennia. It is likely that the area was occupied in pre-Roman times, but the first clear archaeological evidence is a Roman signal station (which has good line of sight to the one at Scarborough) on Carr Naze. This is dated to the 4th century, late in the Roman occupation. Many people believe that a mostly submerged structure, called the Spittal Rocks, was actually a Roman pier, probably part of a harbour.

While there's little direct evidence of human habitation in Filey after the Romans left, it's highly likely that a small fishing village existed here. More definitely, parts of St Oswald's Church date back to the 12th century. Filey grew rapidly in the 19th century, with planned development centred on the elegant Crescent. Arrival of the railway in 1846 cemented its future as a resort. In 1947 a Butlin's Holiday Camp opened – complete with its own railway halt – to the south of the town. At its peak in the 1960s it could accommodate over 10,000 visitors, but it closed in 1983. After years of dereliction the site has been partly redeveloped for holiday homes.

Opposite: The crumbling cliffs at Filey Bay

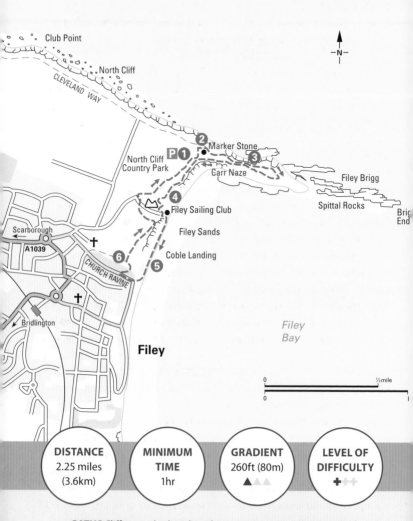

DISTANCE	MINIMUM TIME	GRADIENT	LEVEL OF DIFFICULTY
2.25 miles (3.6km)	1hr	260ft (80m) ▲▲▲	✛✛✛

PATHS Clifftop paths, beach and pavement, some steps, no stiles
LANDSCAPE Windswept headland, sheltered bay and country park
SUGGESTED MAP OS Explorer 301 Scarborough, Bridlington & Flamborough
Head **START/FINISH** Grid reference: TA 123815 **DOG FRIENDLINESS** No livestock
on the route but plenty of cliff edges, so take care **PARKING** Filey Country Park
North (pay-and-display). Out of season there are usually also spaces in Church
Ravine **PUBLIC TOILETS** At the bottom of Church Ravine and at the country park

Walk

1

WALK 1 DIRECTIONS

❶ Go through the gate beside the interpretive signs in the corner of the car park and walk towards a tall pointed marker stone showing the start/finish of the Wolds Way and the Cleveland Way. Continue straight ahead to the edge of cliffs overlooking the North Sea. A small promontory here has good views north to Scarborough, with its castle, and the coast beyond.

❷ Turn right along the cliff edge path, passing the site of the Roman signal station. Beyond this the promontory narrows so much that there's only room for a single wide path. Reach a fork in the path. The branch on the right looks as if it will take you down to the beach, but it's quite eroded and awkward at the bottom.

❸ Instead take the main, left, fork until this too becomes a dead end at a stern warning sign. They're not joking either: the path beyond this point is no longer maintained and runs out onto a very narrow and obviously crumbling ridge. So turn around and retrace, this time sticking to the main path, then follow the edge of a mown grassy area

just below the car park, a few paces back from the edge of the cliffs above the beach.

❹ Where a steep valley cuts into the cliff edge, a marker post on the corner indicates the start of some steep steps. Follow these down to a tarmac lane and turn left down its steep lower end to Filey Sailing Club, then down the ramp onto the beach. You might want to walk along left to look at the badlands cliffs from below, but the main route continues right to another ramp/slipway at Coble Landing.

❺ Go up the ramp and along past cafés, amusement arcades and souvenir shops to the road. Turn right up Church Ravine, then right again up steps near a telephone box. Keep right where the path splits (though it doesn't really matter as all the paths come out to the same open grassy area).

❻ Follow the right-hand edge of the grassy space, above the cliffs, until it turns a corner. Go left above the little valley that you descended into earlier, to meet a road near the Country Park Stores and Café. Turn right along this road to return to the car park.

🍴 EATING AND DRINKING

There are few surprises in the seafront eating places at Coble Landing, or the country park café – most of them are seasonal, too. There's more choice in the town centre, including the award-winning Corner Restaurant and Café-Bar on Belle Vue Crescent. Relying on local producers wherever possible, it offers an eclectic bistro-style menu at reasonable prices.

GRISTHORPE MAN AND HIS LANDSCAPE

A walk in North Yorkshire's eastern extremity, where prehistoric man lived and died.

A little inland from the rocky peninsula of Filey Brigg, which marks the end (or the start) of both the Cleveland Way and the Wolds Way, is peaceful pasture and arable land bounded on the south by the first slopes of the chalk escarpment of the Yorkshire Wolds. It is fertile land, once wet with bog but long-since drained and farmed. The local name for this landscape – 'Carr' – is from an Old Norse word meaning boggy ground.

Gristhorpe Man

In 1834 workmen, employed by the local landowner William Beswick in Gristhorpe, dug into an ancient burial mound on the Carrs near the village. Under a covering of oak branches they uncovered a coffin lid carved with a face (which they later trampled on and made unrecognisable!). The coffin was made from a single oak log, with lichened bark still adhering to it. Inside was the complete skeleton of a man, more than six feet tall, with his legs drawn up to his chest. His body had been wrapped in fine animal skin, secured by a bone pin. With him were a bronze dagger head and a bone pommel for it, as well as a flint knife. By his side was a bark dish stitched with strips of animal skin or sinew. It is believed that he is probably more than 4,000 years old, and is likely to have been a Bronze Age chieftain, who died in his forties.

You will get a fine view of Gristhorpe Man's homeland from the first part of the walk as you ascend from Muston on to the slopes of Flotmanby Wold.

The Carrs

The walk descends along an ancient hollow way route; this may once have been part of a major prehistoric route from the Wolds on to the watery peat landscape of The Carrs. Today The Carrs are criss-crossed with drainage ditches that include the evocatively-named Old Scurf and the channelled River Hertford, which was cut in 1807. To the north is the Hull-to-Scarborough railway line; there was a railway station just south-west of Gristhorpe village. The walk continues by the Main Drain and alongside Muston Bottoms to the village, which is worth exploring for its range of excellent vernacular houses.

Map labels

Cayton

A165

Magdalen Grange Farm

—N—

4

Main

5

6

Drain

CARR LANE

Manor Farm ●

FLOTMANBY LANE

3

A1039

45 ▲

Ship Inn ●

7

Bridlington, Filey

Staxton

WOLDS WAY

Muston

1

75 ▲

2

| 0 | | ½ mile |
| 0 | 500m | |

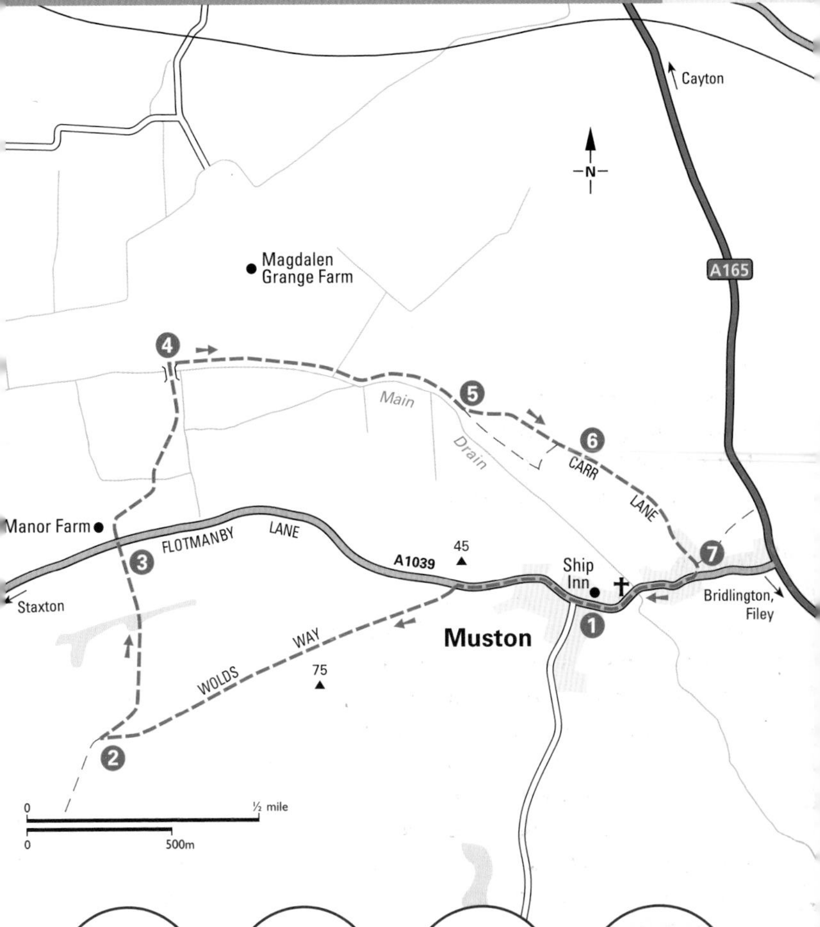

DISTANCE	MINIMUM TIME	GRADIENT	LEVEL OF DIFFICULTY
3.75 miles (6km)	2hrs	249ft (75m) ▲▲▲	✚✚✚

PATHS Field paths and tracks, muddy after rain, 4 stiles
LANDSCAPE Hillside, then flat farmland
SUGGESTED MAP OS Explorer 301 Scarborough, Bridlington
& Flamborough Head **START/FINISH** Grid reference: TA 096796
DOG FRIENDLINESS Livestock in fields, so dogs on lead
PARKING Street parking in Muston, near the Ship Inn
PUBLIC TOILETS None on route

WALK 2 DIRECTIONS

❶ From the Ship Inn, walk in the direction of Folkton. After the houses end, and just before the stone holding the Muston village sign on the right, take a waymarked stile in the hedge on your left, signed 'Wolds Way'. Go forward with the hedge on your right. The path becomes a track. Follow the Wolds Way signs uphill over two waymarked stiles, passing two disused stiles on the ascent. At the top right-hand corner of the next field go over a stile and continue to the next signpost.

❷ Go over the embankment then turn right down the track, following the bridleway sign. Continue downhill, in this hollow way. It comes into a field, which you walk straight across to reach a main road, Flotmanby Lane.

❸ Cross the road and walk through the farm buildings of Manor Farm, bearing right along the track by a barn. The track eventually bears left and crosses a stream, then reaches a drainage channel that is crossed by a concrete bridge with metal rails.

❹ Cross the bridge and turn right at the end, along the side of the channel. Follow the track to the next bridge.

Do not cross, but continue straight ahead, still following the channel. Go through a waymarked gate and continue ahead; the drainage channel eventually swings right, away from the path. Continue through two more waymarked gates.

> **🍴 EATING AND DRINKING**
> The walk begins and ends at the Ship Inn in Muston, which offers bar meals and snacks, as well as Sunday lunches. Just to the north, the Bull Inn in Gristhorpe offers meals and snacks, and welcomes children.

❺ Before you reach another waymarked gate, turn left. Walk up the field side with the hedge to your right. Follow the hedge as it bends round to the right. The path reaches a waymarked gate. Go through the gate into a track called Carr Lane.

❻ Follow Carr Lane between the hedges and past farm buildings. Eventually the lane becomes metalled and passes a row of houses to reach a T-junction before a green.

❼ Turn right, then right again at the main road. Conitnue through Muston, past the church, to the Ship Inn.

> **🔎 IN THE AREA**
> Bempton Cliffs is one of the premier reserves managed by the Royal Society for the Protection of Birds (RSPB), which describes it as 'easily the best place in England to see, hear and smell seabirds!' In the breeding season (approximately April–August) the cliffs teem with more than 200,000 birds.

Opposite: RSPB Bempton nature reserve

GOING TO FAIR SCARBOROUGH

Scarborough's impressive setting is revealed in grand style on this linear walk.

'Are you going to Scarborough Fair?
Parsley, sage, rosemary and thyme...'

Scarborough was an important medieval trading centre and its fair – which lasted from mid-August to the end of September – attracted merchants from all over England and from far beyond, possibly even Byzantium and Arabia. The song, known in various versions, has been covered by many artists, most famously Simon and Garfunkel, and also partly inspired Bob Dylan's 'Girl from the North Country'.

The fair endured for around 500 years, and by the time it finally ended in the late 18th century, Scarborough was already established as a major resort; indeed it makes a strong claim to be Britain's first seaside resort. It was an important spa from the mid-17th century onwards, though the spa waters were declared unfit for human consumption in the 1930s. The Spa Complex remains, its facilities including the 2,000-seat Grand Hall. To make access easier from the town centre, the Cliff Bridge was opened in 1827 and rapidly became a tourist attraction in its own right.

Railways and Funiculars

The railway came to Scarborough in 1841, stimulating further growth. The Grand Hotel, whose imposing bulk looms over the later stages of the walk, was opened in 1863. It was one of Europe's first purpose-built large-scale hotels. Its design features 4 towers for the seasons, 12 floors for the months, 52 chimneys and – originally – 365 bedrooms.

At one time Scarborough had no fewer than five cliff railways, also known as trams or lifts. The earliest of them was the South Cliff Tramway. Opened in 1875, this was the first funicular railway in Britain, and still operates, as does the Central Tramway, just south of the Grand Hotel. The South Cliff lift is operated by gravity using seawater for ballast, while the Central Tramway is electrically driven. The St Nicholas Lift, north of the Grand Hotel, still exists but its future is uncertain; the walk climbs through gardens alongside it.

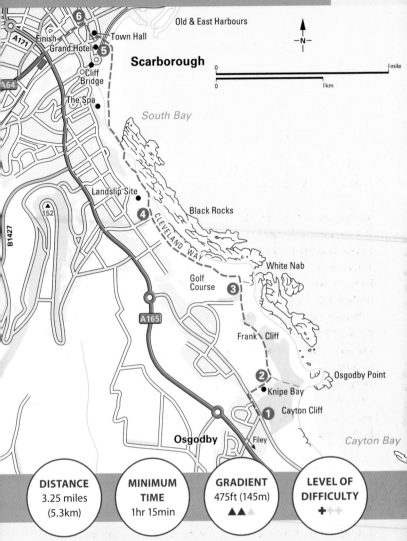

DISTANCE
3.25 miles (5.3km)

MINIMUM TIME
1hr 15min

GRADIENT
475ft (145m)
▲▲▲

LEVEL OF DIFFICULTY
✚✚✚

PATHS Sandy clifftop paths at first, paved paths and streets to finish, with the option of walking on the beach. No stiles **LANDSCAPE** Cliff tops with wide sea views, and seaside town around a striking bay **SUGGESTED MAP** OS Explorer Scarborough, Bridlington & Flamborough Head **START/FINISH** Grid reference: TA 059850 **DOG FRIENDLINESS** Dogs can be off lead most of the way, but not in town streets. Seasonal restrictions on Scarborough beach
PARKING Roadside parking on Old Filey Road, Osgodby
PUBLIC TOILETS Plentiful in the latter stages of the walk

WALK 3 DIRECTIONS

1 From the high point of Old Filey Road (also known as Osgodby Hill Top), walk downhill to the north in the direction of Scarborough. Pass the entrance to the Knipe Bay estate of chalet homes. Just beyond this take a footpath on the right with a Cleveland Way sign, running down between the chalets and a large field.

2 The path turns left at another signpost to run along the cliff tops, although trees mostly mask the sea views on this first stretch. Cross a short stretch of wooden boardwalk before descending a wider track below a small pumping station. Cross a little stream by concrete stepping-stones (usually you can just step across).

3 There's access to the shore if you continue straight ahead, but the Cleveland Way goes left, up steps, to emerge beside a golf course. White marker-posts along here are for the benefit of golfers, not walkers; they indicate the area that's 'out of bounds'. The path is quite clear anyway, and now enjoys unobstructed views over Scarborough Bay. The path traverses the steep slope above the broken, eroding cliffs, eventually meeting a stony track just below a road.

4 Turn right down the track, which runs out onto a wide grassy fan. At the bottom turn left along the sea wall. If the tide is in stay up on the sea wall (with great care if the sea's really rough), but if the tide is out it's better to walk along the sands. Pass below the Spa, Cliff Bridge and the Grand Hotel, then come up a ramp to the road.

5 Cross near the Olympia complex, and just to its right enter St Nicholas Gardens. Go up the steps and ramps, generally keeping left, to emerge near the top station of the St Nicholas Lift. A small, triangular green surrounds a statue of Queen Victoria, and behind this is the Edwardian Gothic Town Hall. Walk down the street to its left.

6 Turn left on pedestrianised Newborough and continue along Westborough, past the Brunswick Shopping Centre. Cross York Road to the bus stops. Bus 7 is the best service for returning to Osgodby Hill Top. Bus 17 will also get you there but by a more roundabout route (it does the same loop in the opposite direction).

🍴 EATING AND DRINKING

Scarborough has a wide range of eating places, from traditional fish and chip shops to fine dining restaurants. Lanterna is a Scarborough institution, garlanded with awards and serving Italian food with a twist (such as polenta with black pudding). Also with an Italian feel, the ASK pizza-pasta chain has an outlet in a crisp modern building in an enviable situation right on the harbour.

THROUGH SCARBOROUGH'S RAINCLIFFE WOODS

Just outside Scarborough, a walk through woodland
leads to the remains of a glacial lake.

The steep hillside of Raincliffe Woods overlooks a deep valley carved out
during the ice ages. Although mostly replanted in the 1950s and 60s, the
woods retain remnants of ancient oak and heather woodland – look out for
the heather and bilberry bushes growing beneath the oak trees.

Paths of the Aristocracy

The woods have long been open to the public, though in the 19th century
they were privately owned by the 1st Earl of Londesborough. Some of the
roads and tracks were named after his family – Lady Edith's Drive after his
wife, and Lady Mildred's Ride after her sister. Lord Londesborough was the
grandfather of Edith, Osbert and Sacheverell Sitwell. Osbert recalled in his
autobiography, *Left Hand Right Hand!*, how he and Edith were taken in the
early years of the 20th century on hair-raising drives by their grandfather in
his buckboard wagon through Raincliffe Woods. They would then walk up
the steep hillsides through columbine and honeysuckle. Unfortunately, they
often became lost, and the Earl's language was, for a time, immoderate, until
he remembered the children's presence.

Best for Beetles

Beetle enthusiasts wax lyrical about Throxenby Mere. The last vestiges of the
huge glacial lake that formed more than 15,000 years ago, after the ice age, it
contains species of rare water beetles, and is one of the places in the north of
England to which coleopterists (or beetle studiers) make tracks. You will also
find the distinctive pinky-purple flowers and wide leaves of the broadleaved
willowherb on its fringes.

   Throughout the walk you will come upon humps and banks, depressions
and pits that show that this hillside has been a hive of human activity in the
past. As the path approaches Throxenby Mere it crosses part of a Bronze Age
dyke system, while elsewhere are medieval banks and the remains of pits for
charcoal burning. You will also pass a small quarry which was used for local
building stone.

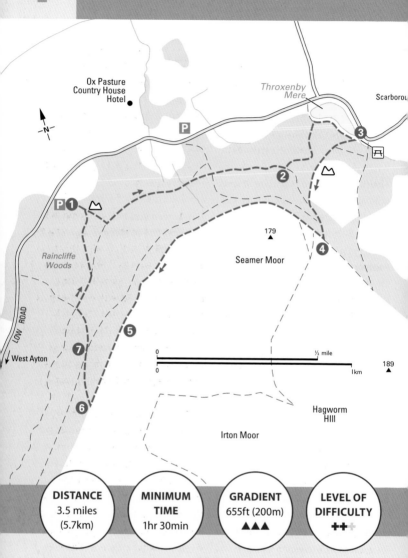

DISTANCE	MINIMUM TIME	GRADIENT	LEVEL OF DIFFICULTY
3.5 miles (5.7km)	1hr 30min	655ft (200m) ▲▲▲	++✛

PATHS Woodland paths and rides, some steep and sometimes muddy, 2 stiles

LANDSCAPE Farmland and hillside woods

SUGGESTED MAP OS Explorer OL27 North York Moors: Eastern

START/FINISH Grid reference: SE 994888

DOG FRIENDLINESS Can be off the lead in most of the woodland

PARKING Car park on Low Road, near road junction

PUBLIC TOILETS None on route

WALK 4 DIRECTIONS

❶ Go up through the car park, bearing left towards a signboard, then go uphill on the path ahead. Where the main path bends right, with green and blue waymarks, go straight ahead, more steeply, to reach a crossing track which runs into a grassy space on the left. Turn left and follow the path. Where it forks, take the right-hand path.

❷ After 500yds (457m) look out for a faint path on the left, which immediately bends right over a drainage runnel. The path goes down into a small valley. Turn left, downhill, then follow the obvious path as it bends right again, past an old quarry. The path descends to reach Throxenby Mere. Turn right along the edge of the pool – this part of the path is on boardwalks.

❸ Just before you reach a picnic place, go through a gate and immediately turn right. Follow the path up steeply, ignoring all joining paths until it reaches a track at the top of the hill.

❹ Turn right and go beside a metal gate, then follow the path just inside the edge of the wood. After about a mile (1.6km) look out for a walled enclosure, tumbled down in places, just left of the path. This is known as Wilkinson's Shed.

❺ The track goes through several clearings with fine beech trees then reaches a gateway (no gate, but a redundant stile); BR is painted in blue on one gate post.

❻ Don't go through the gateway, but instead turn sharp right down a sunken path. If this first bit is muddy, there's a bypass just to its left. The track becomes deeply sunken as it slants down the steep slope. At a marker post there's an opening on the left; walk a few paces to a Forge Woods sign, then go right up four steps and down a narrow path to rejoin the track (this bypasses a potentially muddy section).

❼ The track, no longer sunken, runs across a gentler slope then bends left to meet a broad clear track known as Middle Road. Turn right on this for 200yds (183m) and cross a tiny stream (sometimes dry). Just after this the track forks; take the left branch, downhill. Where it bends left to run directly down the slope, rejoin the outward route for the final stroll back to the car park.

🍴 EATING AND DRINKING

There is nowhere on the route, although there may occasionally be an ice cream van at Throxenby Mere. The Ox Pasture Country House Hotel, not far along the road to the east of the car park, offers dinner in the evenings and a good value Sunday lunch. Otherwise, Scarborough, with its vast choice of eating places, is near by.

BEAUTIFUL CHEMISTRY AT RAVENSCAR

Discovering an industrial heritage amid moorland and coastal scenery.

Ravenscar has a spectacular setting, but what makes it special is its unique place in industrial history, for it has been described as the cradle of the chemical industry. Soon after joining the old railway track the walk passes under high quarried cliff faces, where all around are overgrown spoil heaps. From the mid-17th century onwards, this was an internationally important source of alum (potassium aluminium sulphate).

Decline and False Dawn

The alum industry survived until the mid-19th century, when synthetic mordants were first produced. A rapid decline followed. As the 20th century approached, plans were made to revive Ravenscar's fortunes by creating a major seaside resort. This begin with the renaming of the former 'Peak' to the more romantic-sounding Ravenscar. The entrepreneurs behind the scheme promised that it would be 'the most bracing health resort on the East Coast'. Bracing it may be, but they seem to have overlooked the fact that established resorts like Scarborough had accessible, sandy beaches, while Ravenscar's is unrelievedly rocky. Nevertheless a grid of roads and sewers was laid and some houses were built. Predictably, the scheme flopped and the company was declared bankrupt in 1911. Its most visible legacy today is the Raven Hall Hotel, completed in 1895.

Rails to Trails

The old railway track along which the walk starts was part of the Scarborough–Whitby line, which opened in 1885, and was a major stimulus to the redevelopment scheme. The station at Peak, later Ravenscar, was the highest point on the line; the outlines of its platforms can still be traced. The line closed to passenger traffic in 1964 and to freight the following year.

Soon after there was a proposal to purchase and reopen the line as a heritage railway, but the costs proved prohibitive and many of its backers switched their support to the North Yorkshire Moors Railway. Almost the entire length of the line is now a route for walkers, cyclists and horse-riders.

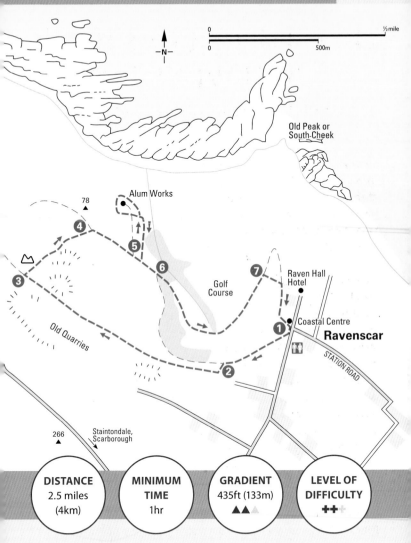

DISTANCE	MINIMUM TIME	GRADIENT	LEVEL OF DIFFICULTY
2.5 miles (4km)	1hr	435ft (133m) ▲▲▲	++ +

PATHS Generally good firm tracks with one short, rougher descent, 1 stile

LANDSCAPE Cliffs and farmland with expansive sea views

SUGGESTED MAP OS Explorer OL27 North York Moors: Eastern

START/FINISH Grid reference: NZ 980015

DOG FRIENDLINESS Can run free in most places, but be considerate of cyclists on the first stretch **PARKING** Roadside parking in Ravenscar, above the National Trust Coastal Centre **PUBLIC TOILETS** By the road in Ravenscar

WALK 5 DIRECTIONS

1 From your parking place, start walking along a broad track which runs in front of the Coastal Centre. (If you've parked higher up the road, you can cut off a small corner by taking the footpath which starts opposite the toilets and soon meets the same track.)

2 Around 200yds (183m) from the Coastal Centre the track forks. Go left and in a few strides find yourself on the course of the old railway. Follow this for 0.75 miles (1.2km), passing beneath steep quarried cliffs. Look out for a stile on the right with a Conservation Walks waymark.

3 The initial descent from the stile, through bracken, is very steep and can be slippery when wet. Continue down more easily, bearing slightly right across an open grassy area before threading through a stand of broom and gorse – this can be prickly for those in shorts! Bear right again across a small field to a stile just right of a gate.

4 Join a good track and turn right. At a junction where the surface turns to concrete, keep right, uphill, for 30yds (27m) then turn left on a path signed 'Alum Works Only'.

5 Follow white arrows down to the site of the works and then continue to do a loop around it, past several useful explanatory boards. Finally the arrows lead back to the main track. Continue uphill on this to a fork.

6 Take the left branch, which keeps climbing gradually, swinging round left to emerge onto a golf course. Keep straight on along the track for 250yds (229m). A green track joins in from the right. Keep on for a few more strides until opposite a black and white marker post on the left (this is not actually there for walkers' benefit, but rather to give the golfers something to aim at because the green is hidden from the tee).

> **ⓘ EATING AND DRINKING**
>
> There's a seasonal tea room on Station Road, open from Easter to mid-October for home-made cakes, sandwiches and snacks. The only year-round option is the Raven Hall Hotel. Its Panorama Restaurant offers fine dining with views to die for, and you can also opt for lighter fare or just a pot of tea in the lounge. (Probably best to change out of muddy boots first, though.)

7 Turn right and go straight across the fairway (after checking there are no golfers waiting to drive off from the tee on your right). Continue up a few more strides to meet another clear track. Turn right up this and out to meet the road on a bend by the entrance to the Raven Hall Hotel. Turn right along the road to return to the start.

DRACULA'S WHITBY

A walk through Whitby town reveals
the inspiration for Bram Stoker's classic tale.

Three of the most significant chapters of Bram Stoker's thrilling Gothic novel *Dracula*, first published in 1897, are set in Whitby. This walk takes you to some of the places where the dramatic tale is set.

Whitby Abbey

The walk starts close to the abbey. The first monastery on the site was founded in 657 AD. One of its earliest inhabitants was Caedmon, a simple herdsman who was inspired by a dream to become a poet. Only a fragment of his work survives, but this is one of the first known examples of Old English, and Caedmon is the first English poet whose name is still known. The walk descends into town by a path known as Caedmon's Trod. However, it's a later Benedictine abbey, dating from around 1220, which stands here today.

World Navigator

Whitby's other famous, albeit adopted, son is James Cook, usually referred to as 'Captain Cook', the greatest of all British explorers. Cook was born in 1728 at Marton-in-Cleveland and later apprenticed to a grocer in Staithes, not far from Whitby. Determined to go to sea, he found patrons in Whitby, which was his home port for nearly ten years before he joined the Royal Navy to further his ambition.

By happy coincidence, his most famous ship, *Endeavour*, was also built in Whitby. In his own words, 'a better ship for such service I never could wish for.' Cook ultimately completed two circumnavigations of the globe, becoming the first man to sail round the world in both directions. On the way he charted the entire coast of New Zealand and the eastern seaboard of Australia.

The walk passes the Captain Cook Memorial Museum, and a memorial to Cook stands on the West Cliff at Point ❺, near the Whalebone Arch. The arch comprises the lower jaw of a blue whale – the largest creature on earth – and has become an iconic emblem of Whitby. The first such arch was erected in the 1850s, while the present arch (the third) was donated in 2003 by the city of Anchorage, Alaska.

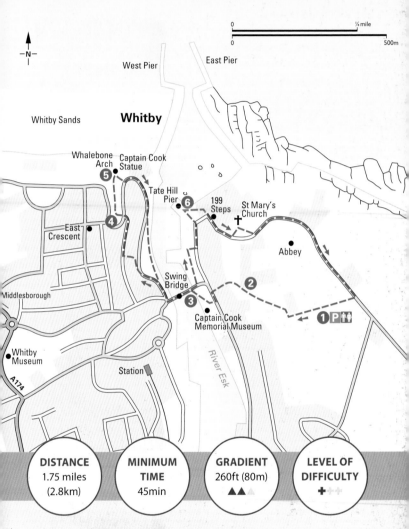

—N—

¼ mile
500m

West Pier
East Pier

Whitby Sands

Whitby

Whalebone Arch
Captain Cook Statue
5
Tate Hill Pier
6
199 Steps
St Mary's Church
East Crescent
4
Abbey
Middlesborough
Swing Bridge
3
2
Captain Cook Memorial Museum
1 P
Whitby Museum
A174
Station
River Esk

DISTANCE	MINIMUM TIME	GRADIENT	LEVEL OF DIFFICULTY
1.75 miles (2.8km)	45min	260ft (80m) ▲▲▲	✚✚✚

PATHS Mostly town pavements, lots of steps, no stiles
LANDSCAPE Old town clustered around harbour and steep cliffs
SUGGESTED MAP OS Explorer OL27 North York Moors: Eastern
START/FINISH Grid reference: NZ 903109
DOG FRIENDLINESS Dogs should be on a lead in town
PARKING Main Abbey Car Park to east of Whitby Abbey
PUBLIC TOILETS At car park, and signed in town centre

Opposite: Whitby Abbey silhouetted at dawn

Walk | Whitby
6

WALK 6 DIRECTIONS

❶ From the bottom corner of the car park, below the abbey entrance, go through a small gate and down a narrow path alongside a field. The path bends right and splits: take the lower path, half right, not the level one further right. Descend more steeply and go through another gate.

❷ Go right for a few paces, then left, to descend flights of steps slanting across a vegetated slope. At the bottom go through a narrow gap between buildings to a busy road. Turn left for 50yds (46m), then cross to a narrow pedestrian street which leads past the Captain Cook Memorial Museum.

❸ At the end, turn left and cross the Swing Bridge, then turn right along the quayside. Follow the road as it bends left then right, then turn left up a steep narrow lane, Bakehouse Yard, right of the Star Inn. At the top, turn right, level at first then uphill again. At the summit, East Crescent is to your left.

❹ Turn right then climb a ramp on your right to a terrace with views of the town. Turn right to find the Bram Stoker memorial seat at the far end. Return down the ramp, cross the road and go up the slope opposite, then turn right to find the Whalebone Arch and Captain Cook statue.

> **🍴 EATING AND DRINKING**
> Whitby has pubs, restaurants and cafés catering for every taste. If you want to sample fish and chips, the top place to go is the Magpie Café near the harbour. Although you are very likely to find queues, the food's certainly worth waiting for.

❺ Descend through the arch and down steps to the road. Turn left and descend to the harbour then re-cross the Swing Bridge. Just beyond, turn left on Sandgate to the Market Place. Turn right here past the little Town Hall, then left along Church Street. As it bends right, go ahead to Tate Hill Pier.

❻ Follow St Mary's road round into Sandside, then turn left up the 199 steps. Leave the churchyard by the iron gate at the far end, bearing left past the abbey to return to the car park.

> **🌐 IN THE AREA**
> Whitby Museum in Pannett Park, on the West Cliff, provides a fascinating insight into what makes the town tick. Run by the Whitby Literary and Philosophical Society, and founded in 1823, it has exhibits of local fossils, plants and animals, as well as displays on the archaeology of the area. There are many models of ships, and you can learn about the history of the whaling fleet from Whitby, and about Captain Cook – the museum has several of his manuscript documents. Whitby men have always explored the world and the collection reflects their journeys.

LITTLEBECK'S HIDDEN WOODS AND WATERFALLS

Walk through a secluded valley to a fabulous waterfall.

Littlebeck is a descriptive name, although by the time it reaches the village, the Little Beck isn't all that little any more. The Beck (from the Old Norse word *bekkr*, meaning stream) is formed by the joining of May Beck and Pasture Beck about a mile (1.6km) upstream. The confluence of the two becks is one of the prettiest spots on this walk, although it's less spectacular than Falling Foss, where the May Beck spills almost vertically over a drop of 30ft (9m). It's nowhere near the highest waterfall in Yorkshire, but it's one of the loveliest.

The approach to Falling Foss is through lush woodland in a deep, sheltered valley. Much of this is now a nature reserve administered by Yorkshire Wildlife Trust. It's valued for its semi-natural oak woodland, which has been largely undisturbed for generations. The oldest trees are around 200 years old. Other tree species include ash, rowan, cherry and hazel, with many alders along the watercourses. Yet this was once an industrial site, and at one point the path climbs over the spoil heap of an old alum works.

The woodland is home to a wide range of plants, animals and birds; the bluebells and early purple orchids in spring are particularly spectacular. However, it is perhaps valued above all for its humid, sheltered micro-climate which supports many fungi, mosses and liverworts. Quiet walkers with the wind in their faces stand a good chance of spotting roe deer, and otters are sometimes seen, especially early and late in the day.

Obscure Hermitage

At Point ❸ the route passes a huge boulder, the interior of which has been hollowed out to create a chamber large enough to seat a dozen people. Known as the Hermitage, its origin is somewhat obscure, though the initials GC and the date 1790 are inscribed above the doorway. Some accounts say that GC was one George Chubb, though whether he did the hard work or merely ordered others to do it is not clear. On top of the boulder are two chairs, also carved out of solid rock, and known as the wishing chairs. The story goes that if you make a wish in one chair, you must sit in the other to make your wish come true.

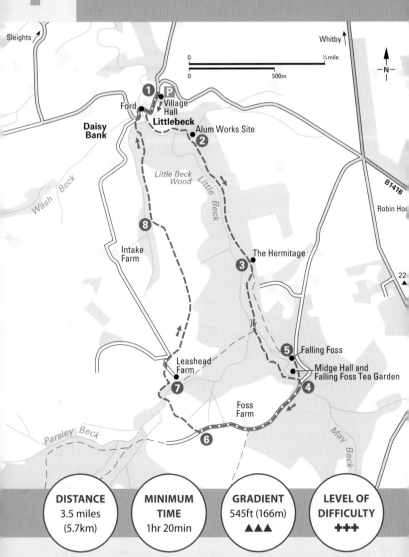

DISTANCE	MINIMUM TIME	GRADIENT	LEVEL OF DIFFICULTY
3.5 miles (5.7km)	1hr 20min	545ft (166m) ▲▲▲	+++

PATHS Some surprisingly rough and rocky woodland paths followed by easier, if sometimes muddy, fields; 1 stile **LANDSCAPE** Deep, sheltered woodland and waterside giving way to open fields **SUGGESTED MAP** OS Explorer OL27 North York Moors: Eastern **START/FINISH** Grid reference: NZ 880050

DOG FRIENDLINESS Dogs can run free in the woods, but the second half of the walk is grazing land **PARKING** Car park (donations requested) beside Littlebeck Village Hall **PUBLIC TOILETS** None on route **NOTE** The best time to see Falling Foss is after heavy rain, but several of the paths can be muddy at such times

WALK 7 DIRECTIONS

❶ Walk down the hill. On a bend near the bottom go left at a footpath sign ('Falling Foss and Coast to Coast') and nature reserve sign. Follow the path through the woods above the beck. Eventually the path swings away in a little side valley, then climbs wooden steps onto a mound of shale.

❷ Descend more steps at the other side, and continue until a gap in a low wall marks the boundary of the nature reserve. Soon the path begins to climb, with some stone steps, to a terrace in front of the Hermitage.

❸ Take the right fork, following a white-on-red waymark. The path descends, with stone steps, past mossy boulders, back to the beck. Cross a footbridge over May Beck, but don't cross a second footbridge over the other stream. Instead follow a waymark and climb a bank between the two streams. Keep following the path, with a few wooden steps and occasional waymarks, until it meets a wide track at a Falling Foss Walk marker post.

❹ Turn left down the track and at the bottom, before a bridge, go left through a parking area to a footbridge. Cross to Midge Hall and the tea garden

❺ Retrace your steps to the Falling Foss Walk marker post at Point ❹. Continue up the wide track, emerging from the woods to fields on the right.

Keep right at a fork to pass farm buildings, and continue to a signpost.

❻ Turn right, signed as a bridleway, and follow the indistinct track through a shallow dip and over a rise. Descend through a stand of gorse, then bear right along the edge of woodland to a gate marked 'Leashead'. Cross a small bridge and follow the track to near Leashead Farm, then turn left at a sign for 'Intake Farm and Littlebeck'.

🍴 **EATING AND DRINKING**

Falling Foss Tea Garden is set above Falling Foss and serves light lunches, cakes and scones. Out of season, there's the Plough Inn in Sleights.

---

❼ Go over a stile and up the field to meet the farm track. Follow this up to a gate, then go through another gate by a signpost. Follow a track down the field-edge to another gate, go through, then turn left along the hedge. Keep straight on, through another gate, until the hedge bends round and another gate leads to the edge of a wood.

❽ Bear right on a green track along the edge of the wood. Follow the track as it descends through another gate into the nature reserve. Continue through the woods to cross a stream and join the lane in Littlebeck. Turn right and cross the ford (usually dry, but there's a footbridge 30yds (27m) downstream), then climb the hill back to the car park.

TIME TRAVELLING AT WHARRAM PERCY

Exploring a deserted medieval village
via some expansive Wolds scenery.

At their closest, this walk is only about 0.75 miles (1.2km) from Walk 9; strong walkers could easily combine the two for a day out. Inevitably, there's some similarity in the scenery, but this walk has some extra ingredients, notably the site of the deserted medieval village of Wharram Percy.

Archaeologists have recognised the locations of more than 3,000 deserted medieval villages across England. Many were identified quite recently, often from aerial photographs, which reveal features invisible to surface observers. Wharram Percy is one of the most important and intensively studied of its kind in Britain. Even here, surface features are mostly subtle lumps and bumps. Fortunately there are some interpretive signs around the site.

Wharram Percy

While it appears intensively farmed today, the landscape of the Wolds was a challenge to early settlers, due in part to a scarcity of accessible water supplies. Wharram Percy is unusual in two respects, in having a large area of relatively flat land sheltered within the valley and in having a permanent stream. The site was almost certainly occupied as far back as the neolithic period, and there is definite evidence of Iron Age occupation. However, it's the period from the 8th to the 15th centuries which has yielded the richest finds. The village was abandoned in the Tudor period as landowners began to feel that they could make better revenues from sheep. Because the site has been used for grazing, and not heavily ploughed, the archaeology remained relatively undisturbed.

Investigation of Wharram Percy was spearheaded by Maurice Beresford (1920–2005). He first visited the site in 1948 as a young lecturer at Leeds University. Recognising its potential, he returned in 1950 and 1951 to dig a series of test pits which established that the 'lumps and bumps' really were house foundations. Beresford teamed up with John Hurst from the Ministry of Works (later English Heritage), and between them they led summer digs at Wharram for the next four decades. Their dedicated work here and at other sites transformed the modern view of the medieval landscape.

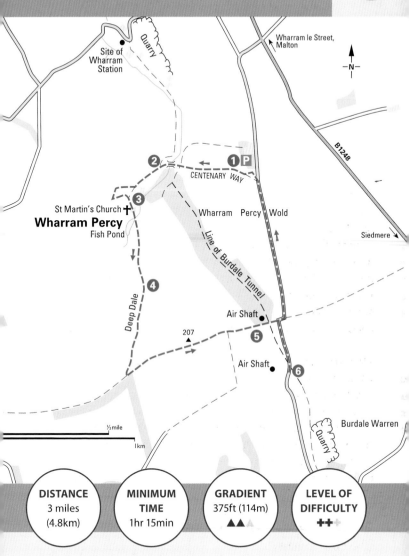

Site of Wharram Station

Quarry

Wharram le Street, Malton

—N—

B1248

② ① P

CENTENARY WAY

St Martin's Church ✝
Wharram Percy
Fish Pond

③

Wharram Percy Wold

Line of Burdale Tunnel

Siedmere

Deep Dale

④

207 ▲

Air Shaft ●

⑤

Air Shaft ●

⑥

Burdale Warren

Quarry

½ mile

1 km

DISTANCE	MINIMUM TIME	GRADIENT	LEVEL OF DIFFICULTY
3 miles (4.8km)	1hr 15min	375ft (114m) ▲▲▲	✛✛✛

PATHS Stony at first, then green tracks, and finally a quiet lane. No stiles
LANDSCAPE Typical Wolds mix of tight green valley and broad open ridges
SUGGESTED MAP OS Explorer 300 Howardian Hills & Malton
START/FINISH Grid reference: SE 867644
DOG FRIENDLINESS There are usually some chances for dogs to run free, but beware grazing stock **PARKING** Small car park for Wharram Percy, signed off B1248 **PUBLIC TOILETS** None on route

WALK 8 DIRECTIONS

❶ Walk downhill from the car park on a clear path signposted to the deserted medieval village. The path becomes a sunken hollow way for a while. Go through a gate and bear right, aiming not for the obvious metal gate but for a kissing gate 30yds (27m) to its right. Go down steps then cross a small footbridge followed by a track (the former railway line).

❷ Go up steps to another kissing gate. Bear left up the obvious track. Where the track forks, go straight up the slope to the level area just above, and the main site of the deserted medieval village. Then follow the track down left to a house.

> ### 🍴 EATING AND DRINKING
> The nearest pub is the Middleton Arms at North Grimston. The view from the road gives no clue to the large and attractive beer garden that's tucked away behind. Food is straightforward and good value, and there are Wold Top beers on hand-pump. In Sledmere, the Triton Inn comes highly recommended.

❸ Go through a kissing gate at the corner of the house and continue to St Martin's Church. Walk past, or through, the church and continue to the restored fish pond. Cross the dam and go right to a signpost and kissing gate. Follow the direction indicated ('Footpath Thixendale') on a path slanting up the hillside.

> ### 🏛 IN THE AREA
> Nothing complements a visit to Wharram Percy better than a visit to Malton Museum, which houses finds from the site and a recreation of a medieval home similar to those which stood here. The museum also has an excellent collection of Roman artefacts from the surrounding area; one of the most striking is the restored wall-painting known as the Malton Goddess.

Where it starts to level off is a good place to look back for views over Wharram Percy.

❹ At another signpost bear right and continue on a near-level green track (mostly tractor ruts) above the curves of Deep Dale. Follow this to another signpost (Centenary Way) and turn left on a green track, leading to a wide crest with views north and south. Pass a bridleway sign on the right and continue along the main ridge track, which turns stony as it passes along the edge of a wood.

❺ Continue out to a road. Walk down right a short way (to the 16% gradient sign) where the descent steepens and there's a view down into Burdale and a large quarried chalk cliff.

❻ Double back and follow the road over the top and down the other side. The lane leads directly back to the car park.

A WALK ON THE WOLDS

From the hidden village of Thixendale over chalk hills and through typical dry valleys.

More than half of this walk follows the Wolds Way, a 79-mile (127km) National Trail that runs from the great bridge over the Humber Estuary to Filey Brigg. At its northern end it links with the Cleveland Way and at the southern end (via the Humber Bridge) with the Viking Way to Oakham in Rutland. Less frequented than many of the other National Trails, it offers consistently fine views and a wealth of archaeological interest along its pastoral route – as well as some very welcoming pubs. For much of the walk, too, you will be following the Centenary Way, a route established by North Yorkshire County Council in 1989 to mark 100 years of local government.

Sixteen or Sigstein?

Some say that Thixendale is named from the six dry valleys that meet here. The more imaginative reckon to count 16 converging dales. Place-name dictionaries, more prosaically, derive it from a Viking called Sigstein. Whatever its origin, Thixendale is one of the most remote of the Wolds villages, approached from every direction by deep, winding dry valleys between steep chalk escarpments. It has a number of old cottages, but much of its character is due to local landowner Sir Tatton Sykes in the later part of the 19th century. As well as building estate cottages, he contributed the church, the school and the former vicarage, designed by architect George Edmund Street.

The Eccentric Baronet

Sir Tatton Sykes, 5th Baronet of Sledmere House, was a great church-builder and philanthropist – and an even greater eccentric. He insisted that his body needed to maintain an even temperature, and was known to stick his bare feet out of the windows of railway carriages to make sure. As he warmed up on his walks he would shed clothing, paying local boys to return it to the house. He even wore two pairs of trousers to preserve the decencies as he divested himself. Flowers were a great hate; he had the estate gardens ploughed up and told his tenants that the only kind of flowers they could grow were cauliflowers.

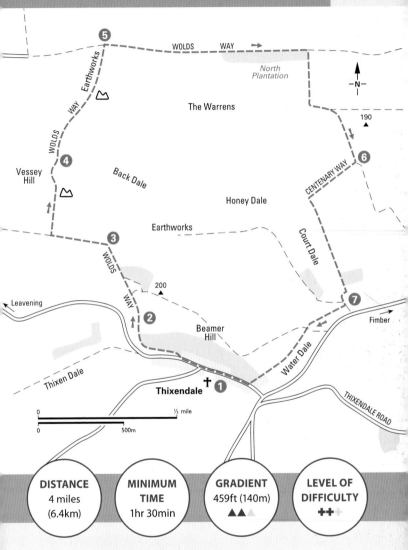

DISTANCE	MINIMUM TIME	GRADIENT	LEVEL OF DIFFICULTY
4 miles (6.4km)	1hr 30min	459ft (140m) ▲▲▲	++

PATHS Clear tracks and field paths, 10 stiles

LANDSCAPE Deep, dry valleys and undulating farm land

SUGGESTED MAP OS Explorer 300 Howardian Hills & Malton

START/FINISH Grid reference: SE 842611

DOG FRIENDLINESS Keep dogs on lead

PARKING Thixendale village street near the church

PUBLIC TOILETS None on route

Opposite: Vanbrugh's Castle Howard is near by Walk 9

WALK 9 DIRECTIONS

❶ From the church, walk west along Thixendale's village street. Just beyond the last house on the right, go up a track, following the Wolds Way/ Centenary Way sign. Cross over a ladder stile in a wire fence on your right and continue walking up the track.

❷ As you approach the top of the hill, watch out on the left for a Wolds Way sign, which takes you left along a grassy track. Go over a ladder stile then straight on along the field side to meet the track again. Continue ahead.

❸ At the next Wolds Way sign, go over a stile and turn left to continue parallel to the track. At the top of the field go right by the sign. The path descends to reach a stile, descends more steeply into a dry valley to another waymarked stile, then curves to a stile by a gate.

❹ Cross the stile and follow the blue public bridleway sign to the right, winding left up the side valley. Near the top of the valley is a deep earthwork ditch; cross a stile and continue along the edge of the field. Where the footpath divides at an acorn waymarker go right, through the woodland, on to a track by a signpost.

> 🍴 **EATING AND DRINKING**
> The award-winning Cross Keys in Thixendale has hot meals and sandwiches, as well as a beer garden. On most Sundays drinks and light refreshments are served from 11am to 4pm in the Village Hall.

❺ Turn right and follow the Wolds Way sign. Follow this track for 0.75 miles (1.2km). At the end of woodland, turn right at a signpost, following the Centenary Way sign to go down the field edge. Follow the footpath past two more Centenary Way signs.

❻ At the next signpost, turn right, again signed 'Centenary Way'. Walk down the field side on a grassy track. At the field end leave the track and go through a waymarked gate. The path goes left and passes along the hillside to descend to a stile beside a gate.

❼ Follow the yellow waymark ahead across the field. Pass over a track and continue to a sign by a stile. Go straight on, to the left of the row of trees. The path descends to the village cricket field. Go over a stile by a gate, on to a lane by a house. When you reach the main road, turn right, back to the start.

> 🥾 **ON THE WALK**
> Wherever you go in the Wolds you are likely to come across earthworks, from large circular barrows to simple ditches. Between Points ❹ and ❺ on the walk is a typical example, a ridge of earth beside a deep cut. It is likely that these linear earthworks were built during the Bronze Age.

RAILS AND TRAILS AT LEVISHAM

Exploring a wooded valley and sweeping moorland skies – and you could arrive here by steam train.

If timetables allow it, there's no better way to arrive for this walk than by a steam train on the North York Moors Railway. Early stages of the walk run through the valley near the line, and later on there's a fine view from Skelton Tower over Newton Dale, where the line traverses what many feel to be its most scenic section. This is more than just a convenient railway walk, however, climbing out of the valley onto moors with far-reaching views.

North York Moors Railway

The NYMR is one of the longest established heritage railways in the UK. The line began as the Whitby & Pickering Railway, opened in 1836. The company was absorbed several times by successively larger companies, culminating in the formation of the London & North Eastern Railway in 1923, prior to nationalisation in 1948.

The NYMR operates several trains daily between late March and the end of October, and at weekends for most of the rest of the year. The company owns more than 20 steam locomotives, some of which are undergoing restoration or repair. The main locomotive base is at Grosmont, but there is an informative visitor centre at Pickering.

Here Be Skeletons?

It's very tempting, when youngsters need encouragement, to tell them they are heading for Skeleton, rather than Skelton, Tower. The name would be apt for this gaunt ruin with its gaping window holes, which stands evocatively above a steep slope overlooking the curve of upper Newton Dale. It's generally agreed that it was built around 1850 for the vicar of Levisham, the Revd Robert Skelton, but there are varying accounts of the uses he found for it. Some say he used it as an overnight lodge when shooting on the moors, some that he found inspiration here when writing sermons. While the tower feels remote, it's less than 2 miles (3.2km) on good tracks from Levisham's vicarage, a distance that would have seemed slight to a country vicar used to walking or riding all over his extensive parish.

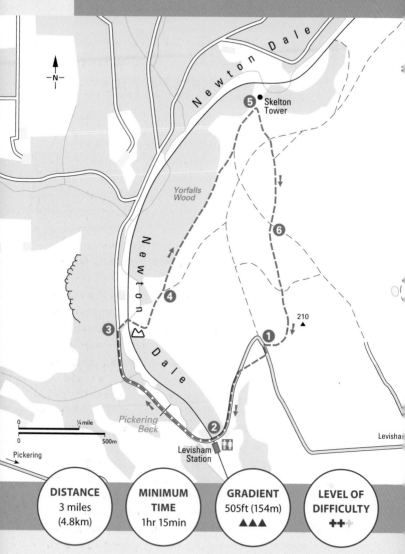

Newton Dale
Skelton Tower
Yorfalls Wood
Newton Dale
210
Pickering Beck
Levisham Station
Pickering
Levisha
¼ mile
500m

DISTANCE	MINIMUM TIME	GRADIENT	LEVEL OF DIFFICULTY
3 miles (4.8km)	1hr 15min	505ft (154m) ▲▲▲	✚✚✚

PATHS Tarmac lane and track, and well defined moorland paths; no stiles
LANDSCAPE Sheltered wooded valley and open moorland
SUGGESTED MAP OS Explorer OL27 North York Moors: Eastern
START/FINISH Grid reference: SE 820915
DOG FRIENDLINESS Sheep and vehicles may limit opportunities to run free
PARKING Roadside parking at big bend in the lane above Levisham Station
PUBLIC TOILETS Levisham Station

WALK 10 DIRECTIONS

❶ Walk up the road to a footpath sign on the right and turn down a green path to cross a stream before rejoining the road lower down. Continue, the road levelling out across a cattle grid before arriving at Levisham Station.

❷ Continue across the level crossing and follow the dirt track beyond, which soon turns back to tarmac. Follow the track for 0.75 miles (1.2km) to a footpath sign on the left, which points right.

❸ Go down steps, across a footbridge, and then keep left for a short way to reach a gate. Cross the railway to another gate. Climb a rough path slanting to the right up a steep slope, keeping just left of a wood. At a couple of waymarkers the path swings back left and keeps climbing to reach open, level moor.

❹ Turn left along the edge of the moor, then continue alongside a wall enclosing trees. Loop right to avoid a wire fence and sheep pens, then continue parallel to the wall until it bends left down the slope. Continue on a level path along the brink of

🌢 IN THE AREA

Nearby Pickering has many attractions, including its museum, castle, the southern terminus of the North York Moors Railway, and Flamingo Land Theme Park and Zoo. Most exceptional, perhaps, is the interior of Pickering church, where you can see what is commonly held to be the most complete set of medieval wall paintings in Britain.

the slope, with great views over Newton Dale, to reach Skelton Tower.

❺ Turn sharp right on a green path running away from the edge of the slope. Keep ahead to cross another green path and begin climbing up a steep slope. The track curves right to maintain a gentle gradient up the slope. At the top the main track bends away left but a smaller path continues ahead along the brink of the slope.

❻ Follow this path along the edge for about 400yds (366m) until another track comes in from the left. This descends sharp right but another narrow path descends ahead. It's a little rough but never too steep. As the slope eases turn downhill back to the start.

🍴 EATING AND DRINKING

There's a tea room at Levisham Station, early in the walk. Another great option is the Horseshoe Inn in Levisham village. With stone arches and a fine panelled bar, plus a grand log fire in season, the ambience is spot on. It's backed up with a balanced menu of contemporary pub favourites, and a choice of well-kept Yorkshire ales.

MALLYAN SPOUT AND GOATHLAND'S MOORLAND

Walking from the popular moorland village of Goathland through woods and over the moor.

Goathland is one of the most popular destinations for visitors to the North York Moors National Park. Its situation, around an open common, criss-crossed by tracks and closely cropped by sheep, has always been attractive.

Spouting About Mallyan

The walk begins with a visit to the 70ft (21m) Mallyan Spout waterfall which pours into the West Beck. At this point the valley carved by the beck has a lip of much harder stone, and the little stream coming from the heather moorland above has been unable to carve its way through. In dry weather only a trickle of water may fall from the side of the gorge into the stream below but after rain it can become an impressive torrent. Take care at all times, and be aware that sometimes it may be impossible to pass the waterfall on the rocky streamside path.

Grouse and Heather

After you have climbed away from the beck and turned on to the moorland, you are likely to find yourself accompanied by the sudden flutter of red grouse as they rise from their nesting sites. Grouse feed on the young shoots of heather, so the North York Moors, which have the largest area of heather moorland south of the Scottish border, are an ideal nesting ground for them. If you visit in late summer, the moors will be clothed in the purple of the ling heather (patches of the rarer bell heather, with its flowers of a deeper purple, and the rose-pink cross-leaved heather, bloom earlier).

Sheep grazing has for centuries been the traditional way of managing the moors; the animals help keep the heather short and encourage the new shoots. Otherwise, bracken, the pernicious invader, will rapidly take over as much as 300 acres (120ha) in a single year if left unchecked. To regenerate the heather, landowners regularly use carefully controlled burning in the early spring or the autumn when the ground is wet. The fire burns away the old 'leggy' heather stems, but does not damage the roots, nor the peat in which they grow. New growth quickly springs up to feed the young grouse.

Opposite: The rushing waters of Mallyan Spout

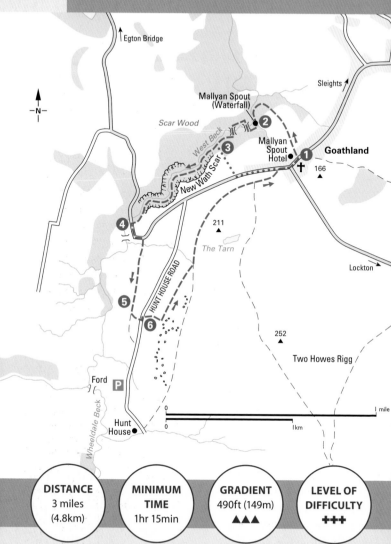

DISTANCE	MINIMUM TIME	GRADIENT	LEVEL OF DIFFICULTY
3 miles (4.8km)	1hr 15min	490ft (149m) ▲▲▲	+++

PATHS Rocky streamside tracks, field and moorland paths, 3 stiles **LANDSCAPE** Deep, wooded valley, farmland and open moor **SUGGESTED MAP** OS Explorer OL27 North York Moors: Eastern **START/FINISH** Grid reference: NZ 827007 **DOG FRIENDLINESS** Dogs should be on lead **PARKING** West end of Goathland village, near church **PUBLIC TOILETS** In Goathland village **NOTE** Without doubt, this is the most challenging walk in this book. The approach to Mallyan Spout is 150yds (137m) of clambering over rocks, rather than retrace this section it is easier to continue to Point ❸ and use the shortcut suggested there

WALK 11 DIRECTIONS

❶ Opposite the church, go through a kissing gate immediately right of the Mallyan Spout Hotel, signed 'Mallyan Spout'. Follow the path to a streamside signpost and turn left.

❷ Continue past the waterfall (take care after heavy rain) and over two footbridges, over a stile and up steps, then continue to a signpost.

🍽 EATING AND DRINKING

As you would expect, there are several cafés and snack bars dotted around Goathland, as well as ice cream vans on the green. The Goathland Hotel offers meals and snacks, and the restaurant at the Mallyan Spout Hotel is excellent.

❸ You can turn left here for a shortcut to Goathland. Otherwise continue on the path for another 0.75 miles (1.2km) to a stile on to a road beside a bridge.

❹ Turn left and climb the hill. Pass a bridleway on the right, then near the steepest part of the hill turn right on a track with a footpath sign. Go past a house and follow the path near the wall, with moorland on the left.

❺ The path bends a little away from the wall towards a power line. Near a corner of a wall just ahead, there's a confusion of tracks. Turn left up the first track, by a power-line pole, and follow it up to meet a road.

❻ Turn left along the road for just a few paces, then turn right up a faint sheep-track up the moor towards a cairn on the skyline. Before reaching this, meet a level path and turn left along it. Meet another track joining from the right and continue until Goathland comes into sight. Pass a bridleway sign and descend to the oad near the church, to return to the start of the walk.

🌿 ON THE WALK

In the valley of the West Beck, and especially near Mallyan Spout, you will see lots of ferns. They are all typical of damp, humid areas, and like every fern, they are flowerless. Instead, they reproduce by means of spores – look under the leaves to find the characteristic dots that are the spore sacs or sporangia. The spores are dispersed by wind or by animals. Each young fern frond begins as a tight curl which gradually unfurls as it grows.

🌐 IN THE AREA

Nearby Grosmont is the northern terminus of the North York Moors Railway and its junction with the National Rail network's Esk Valley Line (some NYMR trains continue on this line all the way to Whitby). Grosmont is also the site of the engine sheds where the historic locomotives are restored and maintained.

ANCIENT WAYS ABOVE GLASIDALE

Historic tracks lead on to wide, open moors and deep, lush woods.

There's a clue before you even start the walk that at least part of it will be on an ancient route. Right by the parking area is a lovely old arched stone bridge over the Esk, known as Beggar's Bridge. Its low parapets suggest that it was regularly used by laden packhorses.

Glaisdale

Immediately after the start, the walk crosses Glaisdale Beck, just above its confluence with the Esk, and then climbs steadily onto a ridge which later gives views of the dale itself. It's a short, curving valley notable for its ancient pattern of small, narrow fields. The field pattern looks almost medieval, but Glaisdale village is largely 19th century. Mining and quarrying have been carried on here for centuries; one legacy of this is the name Delves (Point ❻), meaning 'pits'. The Ordnance Survey map marks 'iron workings' near the track used early in the walk, and in aerial photographs a large number of pits can be seen, though they are less obvious from ground level.

Beasts of Burden

Tracks such as the one through East Arncliff Wood, used in the final stage of the walk, developed to transport stone, iron ore and agricultural produce. In this steep terrain carts were troublesome, and pack animals – 40 to 50 horses and mules – were used instead. Loads would be carried in panniers, with weight equally distributed either side of the animal.

Low parapets, like those you see on Beggar's Bridge, were equipped to allow clearance for such large and unwieldy loads. In East Arncliff Wood, a continuous single line of stones known as a pannier-way runs along much of the length of the track.

Pannier-ways are fairly common in the area, and developed mostly from the late 16th century onward. They were constructed wherever the ground might be soft, to ensure safe passage for strings of packhorses. With heavy use the stones would become hollowed in the middle, and were often turned to expose an unworn face.

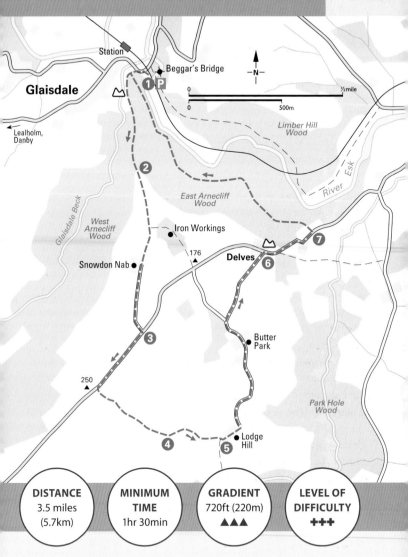

DISTANCE	MINIMUM TIME	GRADIENT	LEVEL OF DIFFICULTY
3.5 miles (5.7km)	1hr 30min	720ft (220m) ▲▲▲	+++

PATHS Good stony tracks, a quiet lane and a short moorland descent; no stiles
LANDSCAPE River valley, sheltered woodland and open moor
SUGGESTED MAP OS Explorer OL27 North York Moors: Eastern
START/FINISH Grid reference: NZ 78054
DOG FRIENDLINESS The track in the early stages and the woods near the end both give dogs a chance to run off the lead **PARKING** By railway arches just east of Glaisdale Station (on the Esk Valley line) **PUBLIC TOILETS** None on route

WALK 12 DIRECTIONS

❶ Walk under the railway. Where the road bends right there's a ford. If dry go across, otherwise use the footbridge. Go ahead up the track. It soon starts to climb steeply, but this shortly eases.

❷ Continue up the rutted track, flanked by well-built walls and trees before open views begin to appear. At Snowdon Nab the track turns to tarmac, though still with a strip of grass down the middle. Keep following it, until it bends left to meet a lane.

❸ Turn right up a steepish climb. After the gradient eases out, look for a footpath sign by a gate on the left. Follow a green path straight ahead down the moor; if the weather's clear, the Fylingdales 'pyramid' on the skyline is a point to aim for. Descend to a gate in the angle of two walls.

❹ Go through and follow the field-edge on the left before turning directly

downhill following the groove of an old track. Turn left in a narrow strip of field towards a house (Lodge Hill).

❺ Go through a gate and continue past the house and various crumbling farm buildings, then follow the access track, which bends left and then right. Continue through another farmyard (Butter Park), and keep right at a fork to descend to a road opposite a thatched cottage in the hamlet of Delves.

❻ Turn right down the road and descend steeply through some tight bends, with a great view of Eskdale.

❼ Just below the steepest section turn left on a track signed 'Bridleway Glaisdale' and follow it through the woods. Eventually it dips to run near the river, then makes a final climb through a gap. Turn right down steps to the footbridge to complete the walk.

🍴 EATING AND DRINKING

Not long ago there were three pubs in Glaisdale, but now the Arncliffe Arms is the only one left, and it's been getting very mixed reviews. There's more praise for the Board Inn at nearby Lealholm, which normally has three real ciders on draft to accompany four real ales. The pub produces its own meat and eggs, cures its own bacon and ham, and gets fish and shellfish daily from Whitby. All this, and they still welcome muddy boots!

⚡ IN THE AREA

The North York Moors National Park Centre is about 5 miles (8km) away near Danby. It's the flagship visitor centre for the National Park, and apart from January and the first part of February (weekends only) it's open every day. Its main exhibition lays out the story of the moors using audio-visual technology and interactive media. There's a fine gallery displaying local arts and crafts, and a tea room.

A LASTINGHAM ROUND

Follow this route from the ancient site of St Cedd's monastery to the attractive village of Hutton-le-Hole.

'In high and isolated hills, more fitted as a place of robbers and the haunt of wild animals than somewhere fit for men to live.' So wrote the 8th-century historian Bede about Lastingham, which he had visited. This was where St Cedd, Bishop of the East Saxons and once a monk from Lindisfarne, founded his monastery in AD 654, and where he died ten years later. Although nothing survives of his church, Lastingham remains a holy place, not least in the ancient crypt beneath the church, built in 1078, when the monastery was refounded after destruction in Danish raids in the 9th century.

Court in Spaunton

Leaving Lastingham, the walk quickly reaches Spaunton. Lined with cottages and farmhouses, which date from the 17th century onwards, it seems typical of many villages on the North York Moors. But Spaunton has hidden secrets; the fields surrounding it are set out on a Roman pattern, and at the beginning of the 19th century a Roman burial was found near the village. Excavations, some 60 years later, also unearthed the foundations of a large medieval hall, which indicated that Spaunton was once an important village, owned by St Mary's Abbey in York. When the estate was sold in the 16th century, the new landowners constituted a special court for the manor, grandly called the Court Leet and Court Baron with View of Frankpledge, which still meets to deal with the rights of those who can graze animals on the commons.

Quakers at Hutton-le-Hole

Reckoned by many people to be one of the prettiest of North Yorkshire's villages, Hutton-le-Hole clusters around an irregular green and along the banks of the Hutton Beck. The village has an old meeting house and a long association with the Society of Friends. One Quaker inhabitant, John Richard, was a friend of William Penn, founder of Pennsylvania. He spent much time preaching in America; it is said he rode more than 3,726 miles (5,995km) and acted as a mediator between the white settlers and the Native Americans. He finally retired to the village, where he died in 1753.

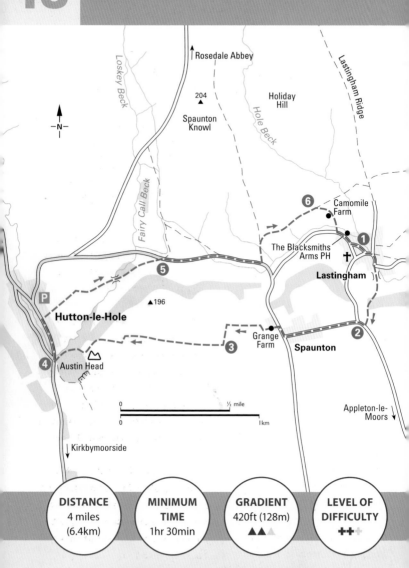

↑ Rosedale Abbey

Loskey Beck

204 ▲

Spaunton Knowl

Holiday Hill

Hole Beck

Lastingham Ridge

—N—

Fairy Call Beck

6

Camomile Farm

The Blacksmiths Arms PH ✝

Lastingham

1

5

▲ 196

Hutton-le-Hole

P

3

Grange Farm

Spaunton

2

4

Austin Head

0 ½ mile
0 1km

↓ Kirkbymoorside

Appleton-le-Moors

DISTANCE	MINIMUM TIME	GRADIENT	LEVEL OF DIFFICULTY
4 miles (6.4km)	1hr 30min	420ft (128m) ▲▲▲	✚✚✚

PATHS Farm tracks and field paths, 2 stiles

LANDSCAPE Moorland and woodland, with views

SUGGESTED MAP OS Explorer OL26 North York Moors: Western

START/FINISH Grid reference: SE 729905

DOG FRIENDLINESS Dogs should be on lead

PARKING Village street in Lastingham, or car park at north end of Hutton-le-Hole

PUBLIC TOILETS Hutton-le-Hole

Lastingham Walk
13

WALK 13 DIRECTIONS

① Begin by the village green and follow signs to Cropton, Pickering and Rosedale, past the red telephone box. Where the road swings left, go right to wind over a small bridge and beside a stream. Ascend to a footpath sign, and go right, uphill, through a gate and through woodland to a gate on to a road. Turn right, signed 'Spaunton'.

② Follow the road through Spaunton, and bend right at the end of the village, then turn left by the public footpath sign over the cattle grid, into the farmyard. The waymarked track curves through the farm to reach another footpath sign, where the track bends left. After 100yds (91m), at a barn, the track bends left again.

---

⑨ EATING AND DRINKING

There is a range of cafés, tea rooms, restaurants and pubs in Hutton-le-Hole – the Barn Tea Rooms and the Crown Hotel are recommended. In Lastingham, the Blacksmith's Arms is a traditional village pub. Lastingham Grange offers excellent dinners and light lunches, as well as a full Sunday lunch, but is closed from mid-November to March.

---

③ After about 200yds (183m), follow a public footpath sign right and walk on to follow another sign as the track bends left. After 100yds (91m), take a footpath to the right, down the hill into woodland. Follow the track as it bends left, then go right, following

---

⑨ IN THE AREA

If you're a real ale enthusiast, Cropton Brewery, 1.5 miles (2.4km) east of Lastingham, is a place to head for. It can brew up to 60 barrels a week, and produces a range of beers. The brewery and visitor centre are open daily during summer, and by arrangement in winter. Sample the beer at the New Inn in Cropton.

---

the waymarks, down a steep grassy path into the valley. Descend to a gate beside a stream, and on to the road through Hutton-le-Hole.

④ Turn right up the main street, then right again at a footpath signpost opposite the village hall. Follow the waymarked route along the field-edges and through five waymarked gates to a kissing gate before a footbridge. Follow the path through woodland to a gate then the grassy track to the road.

⑤ Turn right and follow the road for 0.5 miles (800m). Turn left at a footpath sign just before the road descends to a stone bridge. Continue on the grassy path, going over a stile, and follow the track towards a farm.

⑥ At a signpost, don't follow the indicated footpath but bear right along a green track running just above the farm to a gate by the far end of the farmhouse. Go down a tarmac track to a road and turn left, soon reaching the Blacksmith's Arms in Lastingham.

THE IRON VALLEY OF ROSEDALE

Reminders of former industry are all around you
on this route near Rosedale Abbey.

Rosedale is a quiet and peaceful valley that pushes north-west into the heart of the North York Moors. The village of Rosedale Abbey gets its name from the former Cistercian nunnery, founded in 1158 and closed in 1536. The nuns are reputed to have introduced sheep farming to the North York Moors. Only an angle of a wall remains, containing a broken stairway. Rosedale may be peaceful today, but little more than 100 years ago the village had a population ten times its present size after the discovery of ironstone in the hills in the mid-1850s led to commercial exploitation. As one of the villagers wrote in 1869, 'The ground is hollow for many a mile underground… it's like a little city now but is a regular slaughter place. Both men and horses are getting killed and lamed every day.'

The East Mines
The dramatic remains of the Rosedale East Mines, which opened in 1865, can be seen during much of the walk. They are a testament to the size of the mining operations. The long range of huge arches is the remains of the calcining kilns, where the ironstone was roasted to eliminate impurities and reduce its weight. They operated until 1879, when the owner, the Rosedale and Ferryhill Mining Company, collapsed, but resumed in 1881. The West Mines across the valley had stopped work by 1890, but the East Mines struggled on, burdened by rising costs, until the General Strike of 1926 killed them off.

The Iron Way
The iron ore from Rosedale was taken by rail over the moorland to Ingleby, where it was lowered down the northern edge of the moors by tramway on the 1-in-5 gradient Ingleby Incline. The line had reached Rosedale in 1861, and the branch to the East Mines was opened in 1865. As many as 15 loaded wagons at a time were steam hauled round the top of Rosedale. The line closed in September 1928, and the last load was hauled down Ingleby Incline in June 1929. The track bed is now open to walkers.

Opposite: Spectacular views from Rosedale Bank Top

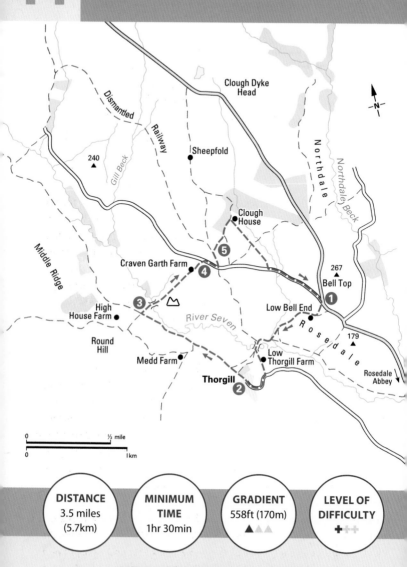

DISTANCE	MINIMUM TIME	GRADIENT	LEVEL OF DIFFICULTY
3.5 miles (5.7km)	1hr 30min	558ft (170m) ▲▲▲	✚✚✚

PATHS Mostly field paths and tracks, 7 stiles

LANDSCAPE Quiet valley and hillside farmland, with reminders of the iron industry **SUGGESTED MAP** OS Explorer OL26 North York Moors: Western

START/FINISH Grid reference: SE 717970

DOG FRIENDLINESS Dogs should be on lead

PARKING Roadside parking near road junction north-east of Rosedale Abbey, near Sycamore Farm sign **PUBLIC TOILETS** None on route

WALK 14 DIRECTIONS

❶ From the parking place take the lane downhill by the Sycamore Farm sign. It bends right. Follow the waymarkers to turn right through Low Bell End Farm gateway. Follow the track through two gates and continue downhill. Near a gate on the left the track bends right, following the stream. After going through another gateway, bend left towards the stream to cross a footbridge with stiles at each end. Follow the waymarked footpath half left, uphill, towards the farm buildings. The route passes through the buildings and on to a farm track. Follow the track uphill, forking right to reach a lane. Turn right.

❷ Continue up the metalled lane, which takes you through the hamlet of Thorgill. Just beyond the buildings the metalled lane soon becomes a track. Follow the track for 0.75 miles (1.2km), going through a wooden gate near Medd Farm and continuing downhill. Pass a small caravan site called Seven Side and begin to rise again. Almost opposite another farmhouse – High House Farm – on the left, go right over a waymarked wooden stile beside a gate.

❸ Walk down the slope beside the fence and pass over the River Seven on a gated footbridge. At the end, turn left to go uphill – a short but steep slope. At the top, the path goes above the stream, generally parallel with it.

> ### 🍴 EATING AND DRINKING
> The Milburn Arms Hotel in Rosedale Abbey offers high-class dining in its Priory Restaurant as well as meals in the beamed bar. The Abbey Tea Rooms provides lunches and cream teas daily from Easter to November – weekends only in winter.

Continue through a gate into the field and walk ahead. Go through another gate and continue up the field with a fence on your left. Go through a metal gate into the yard of Craven Garth Farm. Go through another gateway and pass between the cluster of buildings to reach a metalled country lane at a T-junction.

❹ Turn right and follow the lane; just before reaching the row of former ironworkers' cottages, look for the Rosedale parish notice board on the left. Turn up the track beside it. A little way up the track, before reaching the farm, look for a gate across a track to Clough House.

❺ Go over the stile beside the gate and follow the track downhill towards the wood. The track bends right just before Clough House, then bends left to pass the front of the house. Opposite the building, go through a waymarked gate on the right and walk down the field towards houses. Leave the field by a gate, and follow the track to the road. Turn left and follow the road back to the car parking place.

REMOTE COCKAYNE AND RUDLAND RIGG

A walk in Bransdale from the remote hamlet of Cockayne and along an ancient moorland track.

The hamlet of Cockayne is tucked away at the end of Bransdale, one of the most remote of the valleys of the North York Moors. Here the road loops back into the lower moors, and walking country lies ahead.

The Literary Mill

After leaving Cockayne, the first substantial building you will come to is Bransdale Mill. Here the infant Hodge Beck has been dammed into a series of pools to feed the millwheel. They may date back as far as the 13th century, when Bransdale Mill is first recorded. The current buildings are, however, from 600 years later, when the mill was rebuilt, as the inscription says, by local landowner William Strickland. His son Emmanuel was responsible for the inscriptions that adorn the buildings, in Latin, Greek and Hebrew. Emmanuel was vicar of Ingleby Greenhow, 6.25 miles (10.1km) to the north, over the hills.

Making Tracks

After the climb from the traditional farm buildings at Spout House, the walk takes you on some of the many tracks that cross the high moorland. As you pass the grouse butts you are on an ancient route that traverses the ridge from Farndale (famous for its wild daffodils) into Bransdale. Soon you will turn left along Westside Road. Like most of the main routes in the North York Moors, it follows the summit of the ridge; this one is Rudland Rigg. Westside Road is one of the longest (and straightest) in the National Park, running 34.25 miles (55km) north from Kirkbymoorside to leave the northern edge of the Moors near Kildale. Along its route you will find old stone waymarks and boundary stones. As you leave the track along the ridge, you are rewarded with a view back down into Bransdale.

Much of the north end of the valley is owned by the National Trust, and Bransdale Mill, passed at the beginning of the walk, is a centre for volunteers on the Trust's Acorn Projects – indeed, it was they who restored the buildings. Bransdale has also been suggested as the home of Robin Hood (fairly handy for his Bay, perhaps!).

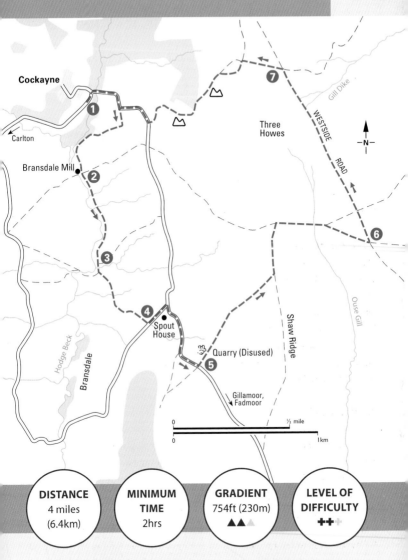

DISTANCE
4 miles
(6.4km)

MINIMUM TIME
2hrs

GRADIENT
754ft (230m)
▲▲▲

LEVEL OF DIFFICULTY
✚✚✚

PATHS Field paths and moorland tracks, a little road walking, 2 stiles
LANDSCAPE Farmland and heather moorland
SUGGESTED MAP OS Explorer OL26 North York Moors: Western
START/FINISH Grid reference: SE 620985
DOG FRIENDLINESS On lead in farmland
PARKING Roadside parking near cattle grid at T-junction in Cockayne
PUBLIC TOILETS None on route

Walk
15
Cockayne

WALK 15 DIRECTIONS

❶ From your parking place in Cockayne, cross the cattle grid and bend right towards Kirkbymoorside. Follow the road uphill and, as it bends sharp left, go through a gate beside a sign 'Bransdale Basecamp' and follow the track down the hill to a gate. Continue along the track.

❷ At the signpost by the crossroads of tracks next to Bransdale Mill carry straight on, continuing parallel with the stream on your right. Go through two gates, following the side of the stream. Climb over a slight ridge to reach another gate. Continue with a wire fence on your right, keeping on the ridge, then descend to a waymarked gate.

❸ Cross the stream and keep ahead. At the top of a rise, go half left across the field, making for a corner of the wall. Go through three waymarked field gates and follow the grassy track along the field-edge to another waymarked gate. At the top of the field go over a stile beside a wooden gate on to a lane.

❹ Turn left. Pass the farm buildings to a road junction and turn right. Follow the road uphill for 0.25 miles (400m). At a bridleway signpost turn left on to the moorland.

❺ Follow the path through the heather to a track, where you turn left. Follow the track to reach a metal barrier. Turn

right at the junction just beyond and follow the track to a crossroads.

❻ Turn left and follow the gravel track for 0.75 mile (1.2km), past a boundary stone and the Three Howes tumuli. Where the gravel track is crossed by a grass track, turn left, following the bridleway mark on the post.

❼ Follow the track downhill. It passes the end of a wood and continues to wind downhill. Go through a gate then bend left along the field-edge to a stile beside a gate on to the lane. Turn right and follow the road back to the start.

🍴 EATING AND DRINKING

The isolation of Cockayne means there are no pubs or tea rooms along the walk. In Gillamoor, The Royal Oak Inn offers home cooking, Sunday lunches and some excellent Yorkshire beers, while near by in Fadmoor, the Plough Inn has a traditional atmosphere and excellent food.

🌀 IN THE AREA

If you're visiting in spring, take a trip over the ridge into Farndale. Along the banks of the River Dove, wild daffodils flower in great drifts of yellow, drawing many visitors to follow the Daffodil Trail. The bulbs may have been planted by monks in the Middle Ages. There's a Farndale Daffodil Shuttle Bus service along the dale, which you should use to prevent congestion.

WARTIME MEMORIES AT SKIPWITH

Discover a wartime memorial,
and a rare survival of lowland heath.

Like Cocket Moss (Walk 37), this is a rare example of a landscape that was once widespread, but it differs in several significant ways. It's lowland rather than upland, and enjoys a somewhat drier climate. It also has a very different history, having been used as an airfield during the Second World War.

Skipwith's 677 acres (274ha) are one of the last remaining areas of lowland heath in northern England. Like most of our landscapes, lowland heath is not a natural environment – left to itself, it would revert to forest.

Grazing Cycle

Today, under the auspices of Natural England and the Escrick Estate, carefully managed grazing is once again part of the cycle of life on the land, and more of the trees will be cleared in the future. The heathland offers habitats to a wide range of wildlife, and Skipwith Common is noted for its insects and birds. Grass snakes and adders are both present. The underlying soil is peat-based, but the wartime runways were laid on a bed of limestone chippings, creating unexpected diversity in a mix of acid and alkaline soils. The damper parts of the common foster an impressive population of dragonflies.

Wings of All Kinds

Birds regularly seen here include several varieties of warbler, including blackcaps and whitethroats. Undoubtedly the most spectacular species to look out for is the red kite. When Skipwith Common was declared a National Nature Reserve in 2010, the ceremony was marked by a fly-past by a vintage Spitfire aircraft.

The Common has revealed evidence of human habitation from 6000 BC. There is little evidence of most of this history on the ground, but you can't miss the traces of its role in the Second World War. These include the remains of a runway at the start of the walk, and tumbledown buildings lurking among the trees and scrub later on. This was RAF Riccall, a training base for bomber pilots who mostly flew four-engined Halifax aircraft. The area around the new memorial, also unveiled in 2010, was used for bomb storage.

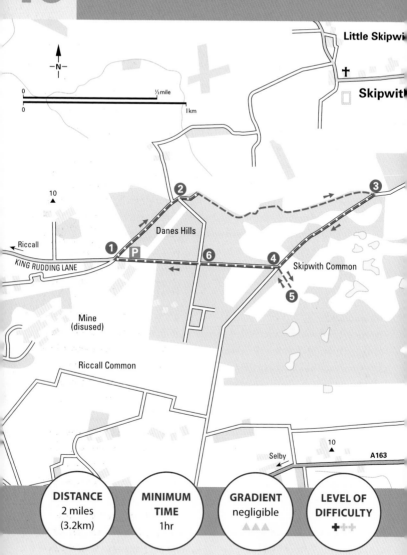

DISTANCE
2 miles
(3.2km)

MINIMUM
TIME
1hr

GRADIENT
negligible
▲▲▲

LEVEL OF
DIFFICULTY
✚✚✚

PATHS Mix of tarmac tracks and sandy paths, occasionally muddy; no stiles
LANDSCAPE Lowland heath and woodland surrounded by rich farmland
SUGGESTED MAP OS Explorer 290 York
START/FINISH Grid reference: SE 644373
DOG FRIENDLINESS Dogs can be off lead most of the way, but beware grazing
stock **PARKING** National Nature Reserve car park at the end of King Rudding
Lane, off A19 near Riccall **PUBLIC TOILETS** None on route

WALK 16 DIRECTIONS

❶ Go through a gate at the end of the car park, near the National Nature Reserve sign, and walk straight ahead down a tarmac path for about 400yds (366m). Wide spreads of tarmac in some places suggest this was a wartime runway. Where the tarmac ends, at a sort of T-junction, go straight ahead on a thinner path into trees.

❷ The path bears right before emerging at the edge of the trees. Follow the edge of the reserve, just inside the fence, with farmland on your left. The path follows the twists and turns of the reserve boundary, crossing several footbridges over drainage ditches, for close on a mile (1.6km). In the later stages, Skipwith's church can be seen away to the left.

❸ Meet a wide track with remnants of tarmac and turn sharp right on this. Now on your left is an area of wetlands. Follow this track for 0.5 miles (800m), passing an area covered in heather with scattered pine trees on the right.

❹ The track bends 45 degrees to the right, with a lesser track continuing straight ahead and another one going

⌖ IN THE AREA

Nearby Selby has a long history, exemplified by the Benedictine Selby Abbey, which dates back to 1069. In 1256 it gained the rare distinction of a 'mitred abbey', giving its abbot a status similar to that of a bishop. Its wealth and power ended at the Dissolution of the Monasteries, but it continued as the parish church and today is regarded as one of the finest abbey churches in England. It is open from Monday to Saturday, and also hosts a range of concerts and other events – hearing one of Yorkshire's brass bands playing in the historic setting is a special experience.

left through a gate. There's a bike-rack near the gate to confirm the location. Go through a smaller gate and follow this track for 200yds (183m) to an RAF memorial in the shape of a propeller from a Halifax bomber.

❺ Retrace your steps to the gate and continue along the main track. After 500yds (457m) reach an open area of tarmac with an iron barrier on your left.

❻ Continue down the main track another 300yds (274m) to a gate and cattle grid. Continue straight ahead to soon reach the car park on your right.

ⓘ EATING AND DRINKING

There's nothing at the common itself, but nearby Riccall has several choices including a fish-and-chip shop, an Italian restaurant and a couple of pubs. Open all day, the Greyhound has a large beer garden and offers a warm welcome. It's regularly mentioned in reviews for the quality of its beer, and offers a traditional pub menu. The Sunday carvery is very popular and booking is strongly advised.

HELMSLEY AND ITS HINTERLAND

Explore a magnificent small market town,
its river and the surrounding farmland

Helmsley is one of the finest small towns in Yorkshire. Its strategic position between the uplands of the North York Moors and the fertile Vale of Pickering is still appreciated by modern visitors, and this walk explores both the town and the beginning of the valley.

Helmsley has an impressive number of independent shops, including a famous toy shop. This is dedicated entirely to old-fashioned toys, with not a computer game in sight. At time of writing the business was up for sale, but the owners were resolved only to sell to a buyer who would maintain its distinctive ethos.

Historic Buildings

Helmsley Castle was begun around 1120. For several centuries it was held by the de Roos family, later passing to the Manners family. In the Tudor period part of the castle was converted into a mansion house. During the Civil War the castle resisted a Parliamentary siege for three months before capitulating. It was ordered that the castle be 'slighted', meaning that the fortifications were dismantled to prevent further resistance. However, the Tudor mansion was left intact. In 1687 the castle was sold to Charles Duncombe, but the Duncombe family soon moved to a grand new house at nearby Duncombe Park, which is also open to the public from April to October.

Nearby Rievaulx Abbey was founded in 1134, under the protection of Helmsley's lord, Walter Espec. There was another abbey near by at Old Byland, but after some dispute Byland Abbey relocated to its present site about 5 miles (8km) south-west of Helmsley. Both abbeys now form imposing ruins.

Walking the Ebor Way

Helmsley is important to walkers as it marks one end of the Cleveland Way – the other is at Filey (see Walk 1). It's also a terminus of the Ebor Way, which this walk partly follows. The Ebor Way is a 70-mile (113km) route which passes through York (Latin name: *Eboracum*); its other terminus is at Ilkley, where it links with the Dales Way.

Opposite: The attractive market town of Helmsley

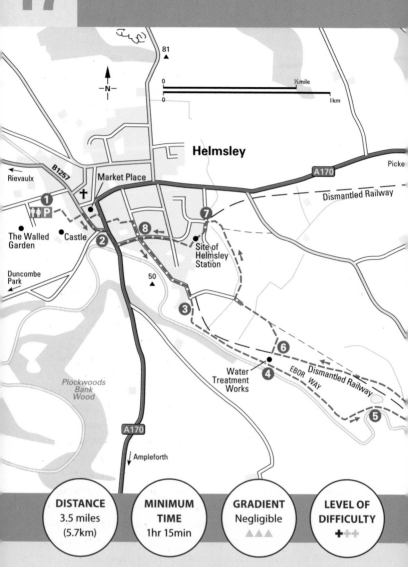

Helmsley

Rievaulx
B1257
Market Place
The Walled Garden
Castle
Duncombe Park
Plockwoods Bank Wood
A170
↓ Ampleforth
A170
Picke
Dismantled Railway
Site of Helmsley Station
Water Treatment Works
EBOR WAY
Dismantled Railway

81 ▲
50 ▲

⓵ ⓶ ⓷ ⓸ ⓹ ⓺ ⓻ ⓼

0   ½ mile
0   1 km
—N—

DISTANCE	MINIMUM TIME	GRADIENT	LEVEL OF DIFFICULTY
3.5 miles (5.7km)	1hr 15min	Negligible ▲▲▲	✚✚✚

PATHS Pavement, riverside footpaths and fields, no stiles
LANDSCAPE Attractive small town, riverside and open farmland
SUGGESTED MAP OS Explorer OL26 North York Moors: Western
START/FINISH Grid reference: SE 609837
DOG FRIENDLINESS Most of the route is either street or grazing land, leaving few opportunities for dogs to roam **PARKING** Long stay car park (pay-and-display), well signed from town centre **PUBLIC TOILETS** At car park

WALK 17 DIRECTIONS

❶ From the end of the car park furthest from the entrance, follow signs to the Market Place. Go past the castle entrance and along a walled path to a gate overlooked by the castle keep. Turn left on a short street, then at a T-junction turn right on a street with a stream flowing down its left side. Follow it round left at the end (Buckingham Square) to the main road.

❷ Cross with care, turn right then left into Ryegate. Turn right into Sawmill Lane at an Ebor Way footpath sign. Walk through an industrial estate, then turn right at an Ebor Way sign. Walk beside the timber yard then into a field.

❸ A track runs along the left side, curving alongside the embankment of the old railway, but the footpath goes straight ahead towards the river then turns left alongside it. Continue beside the river, crossing a couple of small footbridges, then go over a stile and past a water treatment works.

❹ Keep following the river bank until you go through a gate where the trees peter out. Bear left to cut off a big bend in the river, then rejoin the bank and follow it round past pools on the left. Near a power-line pole the gap between river and pool is very narrow.

❺ Bear left to a small gate, and go through more gates to pass under the old railway. Turn left immediately and walk through fields alongside the railway embankment. This diminishes in height and eventually the path runs along the course of the railway itself. At a marker post near a new gate turn right (before the gate).

❻ Follow the field-edge, staying with it as it turns left, to a gate. Bear right to a gate, which leads into a track. Follow this to a waymarked gate on the right. Follow the narrow footpath, then cross a footbridge and emerge onto a road.

❼ Turn left, then go straight ahead through another gate on a path through the site of Helmsley Station. Walk along the platform until the way ahead is blocked, turn right and emerge onto a road near the fire station. Go straight ahead, then take the third right turn onto Pottergate.

❽ After 100yds (91m) turn left down a lane, then bend right into a car park. Turn left in front of Helmsley Arts Centre to a row of shops, including the toy shop. Go under an arch to the main road and cross into the Market Place. Walk down the road right of the Royal Oak to meet the outward route.

🍴 EATING AND DRINKING

You're spoiled for choice in Helmsley, with a clutch of pubs and tea rooms around the Market Place. However, between April and October it's hard to beat the Vinehouse Vegetarian Café at the Walled Garden.

HIDDEN YORK

Through streets and alleys of the historic walled city.

St Olave's Church, at the start of the walk, was founded in 1055 by Siward, Earl of Northumbria and repaired after it was used as a gun platform in 1644 during the Civil War Siege of York. Further along, past the library, look right, as you ascend the steps, to the Anglian Tower. Built on the Roman ramparts during the time the Anglians ruled York (from the 6th century), this building is now surrounded by the exposed layers of successive defensive walls.

Historic Sights

The King's Manor, on your left as you go towards Exhibition Square, was the house of the Abbot of St Mary's, and was appropriated by the King in 1539. The residence of the President of the Council of the North from 1561 to 1641, it was apartments until 1833 and then a school. Since 1963 it has been leased to York University. The Minster Library, approached through Dean's Park, north of the Minster, is the only remaining substantial part of the palace of the Archbishops of York. Built about 1230 as the palace's chapel, it became the library in the 19th century.

Bedern, off Goodramgate, was where the Vicars Choral of the Minster lived. They sang the Minster services, and had their own Chapel and Hall (both of which you will pass) as well as a wooden walkway to the Minster precincts to avoid the undesirables who inhabited the area. Lady Peckitt's Yard is beside the spectacular half-timbered Herbert House of about 1620. After passing Clifford's Tower and reaching Castlegate, visit Fairfax House, a fine town house of the 1740s with its interiors beautifully restored in the 1980s. On King's Staith, once the main wharf for the city, is the 17th-century King's Arms Inn, which has the distinction of being Britain's most flooded pub. Ouse Bridge was, for centuries, the only crossing place linking the two banks of the river. This 19th-century bridge replaced two earlier ones: the Elizabethan bridge had houses on it. Holy Trinity Church off Goodramgate has box pews and uneven floors. On the way back to Marygate, notice the round St Mary's Tower at its junction with Bootham. Part of the walls of St Mary's Abbey, it was blown up in 1644 during the Civil War and later rebuilt, rather inaccurately.

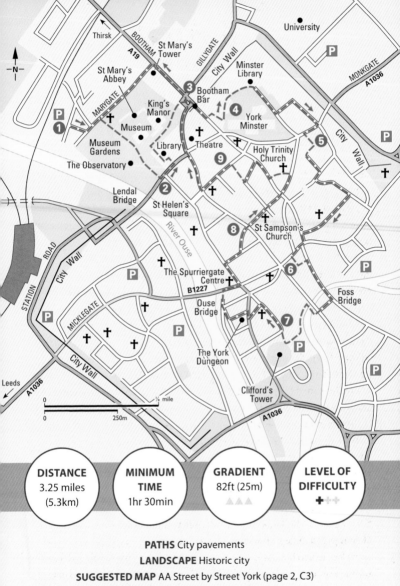

DISTANCE	MINIMUM TIME	GRADIENT	LEVEL OF DIFFICULTY
3.25 miles (5.3km)	1hr 30min	82ft (25m) ▲▲▲	✚✚✚

PATHS City pavements

LANDSCAPE Historic city

SUGGESTED MAP AA Street by Street York (page 2, C3)

START/FINISH Grid reference: SE 598523

DOG FRIENDLINESS City streets, so dogs on lead

PARKING Marygate Car Park, off Bootham

PUBLIC TOILETS Museum Gardens and Bootham Bar

WALK 18 DIRECTIONS

❶ Walk back into Marygate, turn left, cross the road and enter Museum Gardens. Follow the path ahead, passing the Observatory, and leave the gardens by the lodge.

❷ Turn left, then left again towards the library. Go left through a gate, and along the side of the library. Go up the steps, and through a gate in the wall. At the bottom of the slope, turn right and follow Abbey Wall into Exhibition Square.

❸ Cross at the traffic lights and go through Bootham Bar. A few paces on your left, take a passageway beside The Hole in the Wall pub and turn right down Precentor's Court. By the Minster, go left through the gate, signed 'York Minster Dean's Park'.

❹ Follow the path left to the Minster Library building. Bend right through the gate and along the cobbled road. Turn left by the postbox down Chapter House Street, bending right into Ogleforth. At the crossroads turn right, then go left through an archway.

❺ Bear right into Bartle Garth, which bends left. At the T-junction turn right, and then go left down Spen Lane. Opposite Hilary House, go right along St Saviourgate. At the T-junction turn left, then right at the crossroads. Next to Jones's shoe shop on the left, take a passage, Lady Peckitt's Yard.

❻ Go under the buildings, then turn left to Fossgate. Turn right, go over the bridge and then turn right along Merchantgate. At the T-junction, cross the road and take the glazed walkway beside the bridge, signed 'Castle Area', into the car park by Clifford's Tower.

❼ Bend right and go to the right of the Hilton Hotel. Just after the church on the right, go left down Friargate, right along Clifford Street, and left by The York Dungeon. At the riverside turn right, ascend the steps by Ouse Bridge and turn right. At the traffic lights, turn left by The Spurriergate Centre. By the NatWest Bank go right, forking left into Feasegate.

❽ Go ahead to cross Parliament Street and pass St Sampson's Church. Go straight on at the next crossroads into Goodramgate. After 50yds (46m), go left through a gateway into Holy Trinity churchyard, and leave by a passage to the left of the tower, to reach Low Petergate. Turn right, then take the next left into Grape Lane. Where it bends left, turn right down the narrow Coffee Yard into Stonegate.

❾ Go left to St Helen's Square and turn right by Lloyds TSB. Go straight on at the next crossroads back to Exhibition Square. At the traffic lights, turn left up Bootham. Turn left down Marygate by the circular tower to return to the car park.

A PLEASANT PART OF ENGLAND

Hawnby Hill offers a real hill-walk,
but in miniature.

Hawnby is a village of two halves. The lower nucleus, just above the river, includes the village shop and village hall. A second cluster of houses, including the pub, is set about 500yds (457m) away, higher up the slope and tucked in under the steep nose of Hawnby Hill. The walk sets out from here to loop around the hill and return along its crest, a delightfully elegant ridge with great prospects. Like its neighbour, Easterside Hill, Hawnby Hill owes its striking form largely to a cap of hard limestone which is exposed as small crags on the west side of the ridge.

The Hawnby Dreamers

Not only is Hawnby a village of two halves, but the church is detached from both of them. Exactly why the church stands where it does – to the west of the village, forming an almost equilateral triangle – is a mystery. However, the division of the village itself is known. This is the story of the Hawnby Dreamers.

The original village is the higher part, where the walk starts. In the mid-18th century two labourers, Cornforth and Chapman, were cutting bracken on the hill on a hot day. Taking a break, they both fell asleep. When they awoke, the men discovered that they had dreamed the same dream, a remarkable coincidence which suggested some sort of call from God. Soon after this event, they were advised by a Mr Hugill that John Wesley, founder of the Methodist Church, was shortly due to preach in Newcastle.

The three men walked to Newcastle – a distance of around 60 miles (97km) – where they heard Wesley preach, and were converted on the spot. Returning home, they recruited many family and friends to Methodism, but were arraigned before the magistrate for disorderly conduct, and their landlord expelled them from their homes. The Methodist converts built a new settlement for themselves at the bottom of the hill, near the bridge.

A few years later, hearing of this story, John Wesley himself paid the community a visit, recording that the area was 'one of the pleasantest parts of England' – a view with which many modern visitors will agree.

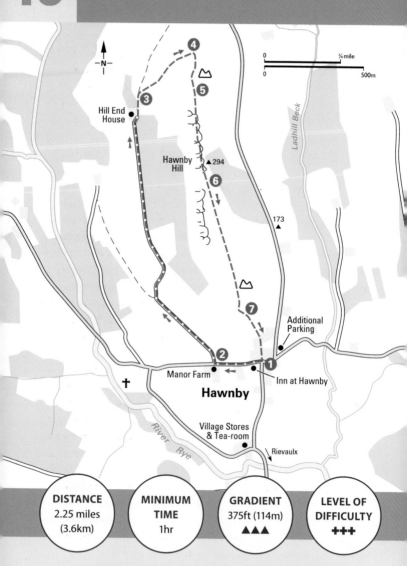

DISTANCE	MINIMUM TIME	GRADIENT	LEVEL OF DIFFICULTY
2.25 miles (3.6km)	1hr	375ft (114m) ▲▲▲	+++

PATHS Lane, farm tracks and moorland paths; no stiles
LANDSCAPE Quintessential mix of partly wooded valley and heathery upland
SUGGESTED MAP OS Explorer OL26 North York Moors: Western
START/FINISH Grid reference: SE 542898 **DOG FRIENDLINESS** Limited
opportunities for dogs to run free **PARKING** Some spaces near road junction
near the Inn at Hawnby, and more just round the corner on the road signed for
Osmotherley **PUBLIC TOILETS** None on route

WALK 19 DIRECTIONS

❶ From the road junction walk west along the lane, passing the Inn at Hawnby on your left.

❷ At Manor Farm turn right up a stony track with a footpath sign. Keep left at the first fork then stay with the track where it bends right, uphill, past a waymarked post. The track soon runs level again, below woodland and past the isolated Hill End House.

❸ At a signpost keep right, following 'Bridleway Moorgate'. After 100yds (91m) fork right up a narrow path; follow it in a fairly straight course between scattered trees then onto more open moor. Meet another track and turn right, climbing gently.

❹ Just before the crest of the rise, take another narrow path on the right. It's a bit vague at first but soon becomes clearer as it makes a grassy parting in the bracken. At a fork go right and climb very steeply for a few minutes onto the north end of Hawnby Hill.

❺ Continue south along the pleasantly narrow, near-level ridge for about 500yds (457m) to the 'summit' cairn.

❻ Follow a clear path, descending gently along the broadening ridge, then more steeply to a small gate. Continue down through bracken and scrub. The path swings left and soon arrives at another gate.

❼ Go down to the right through a field to gates by a small barn and metal-roofed shed. Walk down a shady track to cottages and the road junction in Hawnby.

> ⓦ **EATING AND DRINKING**
> The Inn at Hawnby is perfectly placed for a visit before or after the walk, and fortunately lives up to its position. The menu – available in the restaurant with its excellent view or in the cosy bar – changes monthly to reflect the availability of local ingredients. The choice of hand-pumped real ales normally includes the classic Black Sheep and the more esoteric Sleck Dust from Great Newsome Brewery. There's also a tea room attached to the village stores in the lower section of the village.

> ⓟ **IN THE AREA**
> Between Hawnby and Helmsley, Rievaulx Abbey is a former Cistercian foundation, and one of the grandest and most complete abbey ruins in England. At its height, Rievaulx was home to around 150 monks and 500 lay brothers. As well as the imposing presbytery, the monks' refectory is particularly well preserved. A fascinating exhibition clarifies Rievaulx's story and there's also a café, noted for its outstanding home-made flapjacks.

The atmospheric ruins of Rievaulx Abbey

WINGS AND A WHITE HORSE AT KILBURN

A simple woodland walk leads to the unusual combination of gliders and a massive horse.

Kilburn's White Horse is notable for several reasons. It's the most northerly such chalk figure in Britain (if not the world) and is reckoned to be the largest by surface area. It measures approximately 318ft (97m) long and 220ft (67m) high. It's relatively recent (dating from 1857), and is also unusual for another reason.

Most of England's white horses and other hill figures were made by stripping off overlying turf to reveal chalk underneath, but as you will notice early in the walk, the bedrock here is not chalk at all but older, harder and darker. The Kilburn White Horse was originally whitewashed with lime to make it show up. It is now covered with millions of pebbles, held in place by whitewashed baulks of timber. The horse requires regular maintenance which is organised by local volunteers, supported solely by donations.

The walk brings you first to its head, with ears and eye easily recognised, while from the bottom of the steps you see body and legs but no head. The White Horse is designed to be viewed from a distance. The ideal viewing spot is reckoned to be the two benches just inside the village boundary on the Balk road, but it is visible from much further. The horse was covered over during the Second World War as it was thought it might make a good landmark for enemy aircraft.

Aerial Perspective

The Yorkshire Gliding Club, formed in 1934, is one of the leading clubs in the country. Its location above a steep slope, facing the prevailing wind, is ideal, as this regularly creates the upward air movement or 'lift' that gliders require. The maximum altitude recorded on a flight from Sutton Bank is over 33,000ft (10,000m).

If you're walking past on a day suitable for flying there's every chance you'll have a close-up view of one or more of these launches. The club also has its own fleet of twin- and single-seat gliders available to members and qualified visiting pilots, and trial lessons are available, subject to a maximum weight limit of 16.5 stones (105kg).

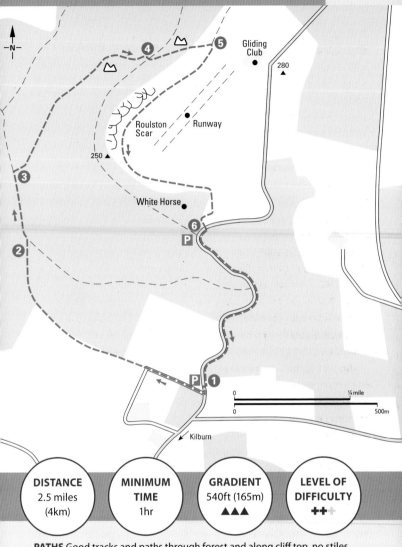

DISTANCE	MINIMUM TIME	GRADIENT	LEVEL OF DIFFICULTY
2.5 miles (4km)	1hr	540ft (165m) ▲▲▲	++

PATHS Good tracks and paths through forest and along cliff top, no stiles
LANDSCAPE Dramatic escarpment with forest below
SUGGESTED MAP OS Explorer OL26 North York Moors: Western
START/FINISH Grid reference: SE 514806 **DOG FRIENDLINESS** Can run free in the
woods, but keep under close control on the cliff edge, especially when gliders are
launching **PARKING** White Horse Bank car park at the bottom of the hill (using the
larger car park directly below the White Horse spoils the surprise)
PUBLIC TOILETS None on route

WALK 20 DIRECTIONS

1 From the car park walk down the road for a few paces, then turn right on a tarmac track signed as a bridleway. When the tarmac bends left continue ahead on a narrower, rougher track. This runs level at first, with fields on the left, then turns into woodland and climbs to a metal barrier.

2 Just above this meet a forest track and turn left. Keep straight on where another track branches right, then in another 50yds (46m), just past a small pool, turn right on a rougher path with a bridleway waymark.

3 Follow this path, climbing gently, keeping straight on across a partially overgrown forest track by another bridleway signpost. The track soon bends right and climbs more steeply before meeting another track which runs fairly level across the slope. Turn right on this track for a few paces, then go left to join another, narrower, path which slants up the slope.

4 Go past a bench and the path starts to climb more steeply. It becomes quite rocky, but not difficult, and there are handrails on the left for much of the

way. The path slants across a steep slope with some outcrops of rock before emerging on the level cliff top.

5 Turn right on a gravelled path skirting the glider field. Follow the path above Roulston Scar and Ivy Scar to reach the head of the White Horse. Follow railings skirting just above the horse's back, then go down steep steps by its back legs to reach the main White Horse car park.

6 From the car park entrance go across the road to a narrow path through the trees. Just a few paces in is a path which runs downhill, keeping parallel to the road. This leads back to the bottom of the hill and the start.

WANDERINGS FROM OSMOTHERLEY

Rambling through fields, woods and waterside, poised between the North York Moors and the broad lowlands.

Osmotherley is a fine North York Moors village, though 'handsome' is a better description for it than 'pretty'. It stands near the north-west extremity of the National Park, and as the walk climbs away from the village it soon traverses a hillside with splendid views, not of the moors, but over the wide Vale of Mowbray to the hills of the Yorkshire Dales. The moors come into view later as the walk turns east, over a ridge, before descending to Cod Beck Reservoir.

Walkers' Junction
Osmotherley is a significant place for walkers. Here the Cleveland Way (see Walk 1) intersects with the Coast to Coast Walk. The 190-mile (306km) Coast to Coast route, from St Bees in Cumbria to Robin Hood's Bay, was the brainchild of walker and guidebook author A Wainwright (1907–91).

Osmotherley is also the start point of the Lyke Wake Walk. This originated in 1955 following a claim by local farmer, Bill Cowley, that one could walk 40 miles (64km) across the North York Moors, all on heather bar a few road crossings. This became an extremely popular challenge, with large groups of walkers attempting the route. Inevitably this led to serious erosion. Today the Lyke Wake Club works with landowners and the National Park authorities to try and spread the load. Mass-participation events are no longer promoted. There's no officially-defined route – the aim is simply to link the two end points, keeping to the high ground (essentially the main watershed of the moors). The official western terminus is the Lyke Wake Stone, by the minor road just north of Cod Beck Reservoir. This walk overlooks the opening stages as it descends towards Point ❺. The eastern end-point is the Raven Hall Hotel at Ravenscar (see Walk 5).

Walking with the Grain
The Lyke Wake Walk is usually done from west to east. As the prevailing wind is from the west, this generally means you have the wind behind you. Heather also tends to grow away from the wind and therefore provides less resistance – a useful tip when planning any moorland walk.

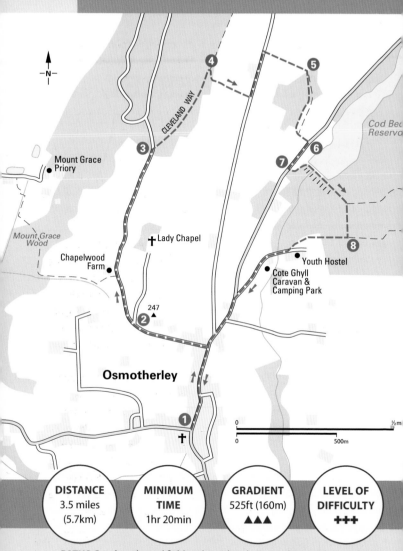

Mount Grace Priory

Mount Grace Wood

CLEVELAND WAY

Cod Beck Reservoir

Chapelwood Farm

+ Lady Chapel

247

Youth Hostel

Cote Ghyll Caravan & Camping Park

Osmotherley

0 ½m
0 500m

DISTANCE	MINIMUM TIME	GRADIENT	LEVEL OF DIFFICULTY
3.5 miles (5.7km)	1hr 20min	525ft (160m) ▲▲▲	+++

PATHS Good tracks and field paths with a short rougher section, 1 stile

LANDSCAPE Village, upland pasture and forest

SUGGESTED MAP OS Explorer OL26 North York Moors: Western

START/FINISH Grid reference: SE 456972

DOG FRIENDLINESS Opportunities for dogs to run on enclosed tracks and in forest **PARKING** Roadside parking in Osmotherley; the nearer the 'Top End' you park, the shorter the walk **PUBLIC TOILETS** Osmotherley, just south of centre (and voted the best in the UK more than once)

WALK 21 DIRECTIONS

❶ From the centre of the village walk up the road signed for Cote Ghyll Caravan Park and Youth Hostel. At the top of the rise turn left on a track with a Cleveland Way sign to Scarth Nick. The track gains a tarmac surface as it climbs a rise, then turns stony as it continues around the hill.

❷ Keep left at a fork (the right branch is signed 'Footpath Lady Chapel'). The stony track ends near Chapelwood Farm; continue along a green track with a hedge on the left. Go through fields to a gate into woods.

❸ A few paces further on the track forks; take the right branch, still following the Cleveland Way. Follow the track, climbing gently. Near the top it bends right to climb more steeply. As it starts to bend back left, look for a narrow, level path on the right.

❹ Follow this path, soon bending left to a field gate. Follow the left edge of the field to meet a walled track. Turn left and go past some agricultural buildings, then turn right at a footpath sign. Go down by the wall to a stile and follow the path through bracken.

❺ As the path descends more steeply, above a small valley on the left, it becomes a little confusing. The clearest path goes left, but this leads away from the right of way. Instead keep right, keeping the wet ground in the bottom of the small valley to your left. Descend gradually to meet a stone wall running across the slope and follow this along to the right. Go through a gap in a crossing wall, then turn down left on a rather wet track to meet a road.

❻ Cod Beck Reservoir is just below but there's no direct access to it. Instead turn right along the road to a gate into the reservoir grounds.

❼ Cross the dam and follow a track ahead into forest. After 100yds (91m) pass a waymark post and a narrow path on the right; 30yds (27m) further on there's a wider path on the right. Follow this for about 200yds (183m) to meet another footpath and turn right.

❽ The path runs down to a kissing gate and just below this meets a tarmac track near a whitewashed building, Osmotherley Youth Hostel. Continue down the track, passing the entrance to Cote Ghyll Caravan & Camping Park, and go up slightly to meet a road. Turn left and follow the road back into Osmotherley.

🍴 EATING AND DRINKING
Osmotherley has a choice of pubs. The Three Tuns stands out as being just a little bit different. The Rennie Mackintosh-inspired decor makes a refreshing change and the menu is also fresh and original, with a terrific sandwich selection using local, craft-baked bread and fresh ingredients.

JAMES HERRIOT'S 'DARROWBY'

Writer and vet James Herriot based his fictional home
town on his real one – the market town of Thirsk.

The elegant Georgian village street of Sowerby – now joined on to the town
of Thirsk – is lined with a handsome avenue of lime trees. Such a civilised
aspect belies the origins of the village's name, for Sowerby means the
'township in the muddy place'. Once you begin the walk, the reason becomes
evident, even in dry weather. Sowerby is on the edge of the flood plain of the
Cod Beck. Sowerby Flatts, which you will see across the beck at the start of
the walk, and cross at the finish, is a popular venue for impromptu games of
football and other sports, but is still prone to flooding.

Between Old and New

Once you've crossed the road by the end of New Bridge, you are walking
between Old Thirsk and New Thirsk – though new in this context still means
medieval. Old Thirsk is set to the east of the Cod Beck. Like Sowerby, it too has
a watery name, for Thirsk comes from an old Swedish word meaning a 'fen'.
New Thirsk, to the west, is centred on the cobbled market place. The Parish
Church of St Mary is the best Perpendicular church in the county, and is
frequently called the 'cathedral of North Yorkshire'. It was built between 1420
and 1480, with few significant alterations since. It was extensively restored in
1876. There's no admission charge, but donations are invited.

'Darrowby' and Wight

For many visitors, the essential place to visit in Thirsk is Skeldale House in
Kirkgate – on the right as you return from the church to the Market Square.
This was the surgery of local vet James Wight (1916–95) – better known by
his pen name, James Herriot. Now an award-winning museum, The World of
James Herriot, this was where Wight worked for all his professional life. Thirsk
itself is a major character in the popular books, appearing lightly disguised
as 'Darrowby'. The museum has reconstructions of what the surgery and the
family rooms were like in the 1940s, and tells the history of veterinary science.
Whether or not you're a fan of the Herriot tales, which began with *If Only They
Could Talk* in 1970, you'll find it a fascinating and nostalgic tour.

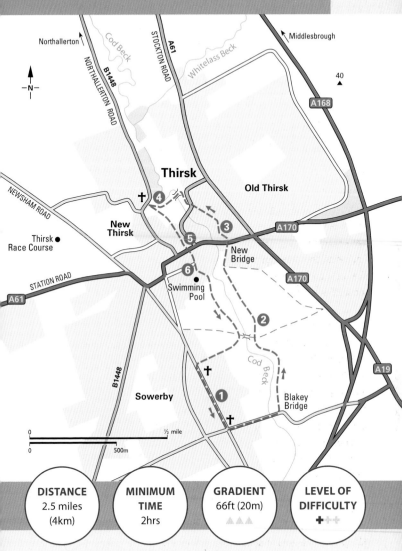

DISTANCE
2.5 miles
(4km)

MINIMUM TIME
2hrs

GRADIENT
66ft (20m)
▲▲▲

LEVEL OF DIFFICULTY
✚✚✚

PATHS Town paths, field paths and tracks, 1 stile
LANDSCAPE Streamside and undulating pastureland around town
SUGGESTED MAP OS Explorer 302 Northallerton & Thirsk
START/FINISH Grid reference: SE 430813
DOG FRIENDLINESS Keep dogs on lead
PARKING Roadside parking in the main street of Sowerby
PUBLIC TOILETS Thirsk town centre

WALK 22 DIRECTIONS

❶ Walk down the village street, away from Thirsk. Just past the Methodist church on the left, go left down Blakey Lane. Cross the bridge, turn left on a signed path and follow the stream, going through two kissing gates to a footbridge.

❷ Continue beside the stream to a stile. Go through two gates to a car park and ahead to a main road. Cross, and take a path running down beside the bridge then curving right to follow the river bank. At a paved area, bear right to join a road beside a green. Follow the road round left, with a larger green area on your right.

🍴 EATING AND DRINKING
Thirsk has a good choice of cafés, pubs and hotels. Recommended are the up-market Golden Fleece in the Market Place and the Lord Nelson. Yorks Tea Rooms, also in the Market Place, offers good lunches and a range of coffees. In Sowerby, both Sheppard's Hotel and Restaurant and Oswalds offer lunch and dinner.

❸ Keep straight on to reach another green – this one is called simply The Green – and continue ahead, crossing a main road. At the top of The Green go left down a footpath to a metal bridge. Cross and continue straight ahead on a path with white railings, beside the beck, to a green area near the church.

🔎 IN THE AREA
Visit the Thirsk Museum and tourist information centre at 14 Kirkgate. As well as having interesting local exhibits and displays, this was the birthplace, in November 1756, of Thomas Lord. The son of a local farmer, Lord made his name as a professional cricketer, and set up his own ground in Dorset Square, London, in 1787. Lord's Cricket Ground moved to its present site in 1814.

❹ Go ahead to take a look at the church, then double back almost completely to walk down Marage Road to car and coach parks. Bear right following pedestrian signs for 'Town Centre' and, as the lane bends round to the right, go down an alley on the left.

❺ Emerge into a pedestrianised street. Go straight ahead again through another narrow alley to reach the Market Place opposite the clock tower. Go straight across towards the Golden Fleece. Go down a signed passageway two premises to the left of the pub, cross a lane and go down Villa Place.

❻ Bear left to pass the swimming pool. Turn right and bend round the pool building to reach a gate. Go ahead to a gate and parallel with the beck. At the bridge, turn right across the field on a grassy track to a gate onto a lane, then continue straight ahead back to Sowerby.

AROUND ANCIENT ISURIUM BRIGANTIUM

A riverside stroll at Aldborough, from the site of an important Roman town.

The River Ure shows a lively character in Wensleydale, tumbling over cascades (as seen on Walk 29). Thirty-five miles (56km) downstream it winds in leisurely fashion through a broad flood plain where stand the town of Boroughbridge and the adjacent village of Aldborough.

The River Ure is navigable above Boroughbridge thanks to the Milby Cut, a short canal completed in 1789 to bypass the weir. (Navigation continues as far as the outskirts of Ripon.) The entrance of the Cut and the lock gates are seen across the river near Point ❺. Boat trips are advertised from Boroughbridge.

Site of a Stronghold

The 'borough' element in both place-names was originally 'burg', meaning stronghold. Boroughbridge is the 'bridge near the stronghold', and Aldborough simply 'old stronghold'. Aldborough was an important Roman, or perhaps more properly Romano-British, centre. Known as *Isurium*, or *Isurium Brigantium*, it was the principal town of the Brigantes, the largest British tribe. The Romans subdued the Brigantes in the last quarter of the 1st century AD and established Isurium as an administrative centre.

Much of the Roman site is overlain by present-day Aldborough. The boundaries of the village largely coincide with the ancient perimeter, and the map of the village still shows strong traces of a grid pattern. It's thought, for instance, that the present church stands on the site of a Roman temple, probably dedicated to the god Mercury.

Later development means that relatively little of the fabric of the Romano-British town survives, apart from a small area at the south-west end of the village, managed by English Heritage. You can view some fragments of wall and an interesting small museum, but the great treasure is found at the far end of the site. Here are two superb mosaic floors, still in situ, with one in almost pristine condition. Both were buried for 1,500 years before being uncovered in the 19th century. It really does send tingles down the spine to think of sandalled feet walking across that floor almost two thousand years ago

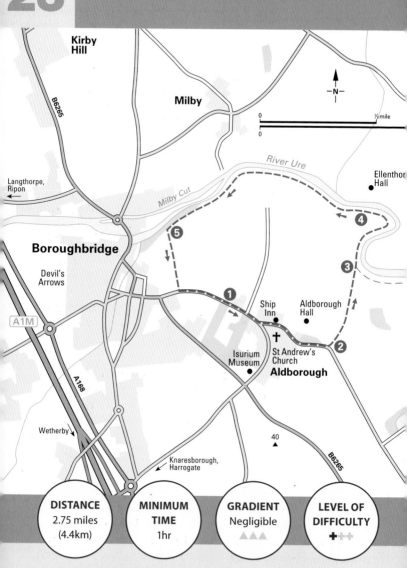

DISTANCE
2.75 miles
(4.4km)

MINIMUM TIME
1hr

GRADIENT
Negligible
▲▲▲

LEVEL OF DIFFICULTY
✚✚✚

PATHS Lanes and easy field paths along an embankment; no stiles
LANDSCAPE Pretty village and level riverside farmland
SUGGESTED MAP OS Explorer 299 Ripon & Boroughbridge
START/FINISH Grid reference: SE 405664 **DOG FRIENDLINESS** Dogs may run free
if there is no grazing stock in the riverside fields
PARKING Space on roadside in Aldborough
PUBLIC TOILETS Back Lane Car Park, Boroughbridge

WALK 23 DIRECTIONS

❶ Walk down the road through the village, leaving the tall Battle Cross and St Andrew's Church to your right and passing the Ship Inn on your left. Walk along a brick wall and tall yew hedge, which conceal Aldborough Hall from the road.

❷ At the end of the yew hedge turn left on a surfaced track, with open fields on the right. Soon there's a view of Aldborough Hall on the left, and then there are fields both sides.

🌿 ON THE WALK

Walking along the yew hedge towards Point **❷**, remember that the tempting red berries of the yew are poisonous. Strictly speaking, it's the seed within that's poisonous, not the red flesh. The yew is a slow-growing but very long-lived tree; the exact age of the oldest specimens is hard to determine but some yews are almost certainly over 2,000 years old. Yews are often found in churchyards, and there are several at St Andrew's in Aldborough. Famously, yew wood is the best for making longbows.

⌖ IN THE AREA

A few miles away in Knaresborough, Mother Shipton's Cave and its Petrifying Well are claimed to be the oldest tourist attraction in England. The original Mother Shipton was apparently born illegitimately in the cave in 1488, but became regarded as a prophetess. She died in 1561, and her foretellings were preserved solely by word of mouth for 80 years before first being transcribed.

❸ At the end of the track turn left on a clear path along the top of the embankment, just above the river. Follow this path around a big bend in the river. Its course becomes straighter as you pass Ellenthorpe Hall on the opposite bank.

❹ About 0.5 miles (800m) further on pass the entrance to the Milby Cut, with its lock gates, on the far side of the river. Continue for another 400yds (366m) until the way ahead is emphatically blocked by a metal fence and locked gate.

❺ Go down to the left and follow the path between fields and out to the road. Turn left to return to the starting point and your car.

🍽 EATING AND DRINKING

Viewers of television's 'Ramsay's Kitchen Nightmares' may recall the Fenwick Arms in North Lancashire, which became the home of 'The Campaign for Real Gravy'. That campaign, and the former licensees of the Fenwick Arms, are now based at Aldborough's Ship Inn. Naturally, roast beef and Yorkshire pudding are at the top of the menu and there's a warm, if sometimes slightly eccentric, welcome.

A GARDENER'S DELIGHT IN HARROGATE

An easy linear walk leads from Harrogate town centre through Valley Gardens to Harlow Carr Gardens.

Harrogate's civic motto is *'Arx celebris fontibus'*, usually translated as 'a citadel famous for its springs'. This is very apt for the most important spa town in northern England, and one of the most famous in the whole country.

A Good Sort of Purge

Visitors began to come in numbers after the publication of *Spadacrene Anglica*, or the *English Spa Fountain*, by Edmund Deane of York, in 1626. Sulphur-rich wells were also discovered and a number of inns were built. The spas continued to be a mainstay of Harrogate's economy for over a century, but decline set in during the 1960s. With large numbers of hotel beds to fill, Harrogate rebranded itself as a major conference destination and gained abundant early publicity by hosting the Eurovision Song Contest in the same year. Today it's one of the largest conference and exhibition centres in the UK.

Valley Gardens and Harlow Carr

Harrogate's Valley Gardens were laid out in stages during the second half of the 19th century. They centre on the area known as Bog's Field, where no fewer than 36 mineral springs have been identified; no two are exactly alike, creating a diversity unique in the world. The formal gardens lead on to the Pinewoods, which feel wild by comparison. Come here early in the day and walk quietly, and you may spot a fox or roe deer.

The gardens at Harlow Carr also owe their development to sulphur springs. A bathouse and hotel (now the Harrogate Arms) were built in the 1840s. The gardens were acquired by the Northern Horticultural Society and opened as a botanical garden in 1950, principally to study the viability of plants in this northern, elevated site. Geoffrey Smith, famous from BBC radio's 'Gardener's Question Time', was Superintendent of Harlow Carr from 1954 to 1974.

The Northern Horticultural Society amalgamated with the Royal Horticultural Society in 2001. The six well-heads by the bathouse (now a study centre) were capped but remain under the limestone rock garden, and the smell of sulphur can be quite distinct, especially on still days.

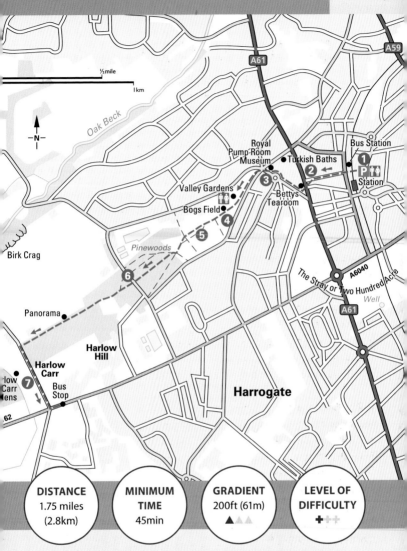

DISTANCE	MINIMUM TIME	GRADIENT	LEVEL OF DIFFICULTY
1.75 miles (2.8km)	45min	200ft (61m) ▲▲▲	✚✚✚

PATHS Streets, tarmac paths and good woodland paths, no stiles
LANDSCAPE Town, park and woodland with some open views
SUGGESTED MAPS OS Explorer 289 Leeds or 297 Lower Wharfedale
& Washburn Valley **START/FINISH** Grid reference: SE 303553
DOG FRIENDLINESS Well-behaved dogs maay be off the lead in the Pinewoods
PARKING Victoria multi-storey car park
PUBLIC TOILETS Victoria car park and Valley Gardens

WALK 24 DIRECTIONS

❶ From Level 10 of the car park follow the covered walkway to Victoria Gardens Shopping Centre. Descend to street level and exit onto Cambridge Street and turn left. Cambridge Street is also easily accessed from the bus station (turn left along Station Parade, then right into Cambridge Street) and from the railway station (right and then left).

❷ Cambridge Street opens into a square. Cross a zebra crossing, pass right of the war memorial, and cross another crossing and go down the street ahead, just left of Bettys tea room. At the bottom follow the pavement round right to another zebra crossing and walk in front of the Crown Hotel.

❸ Pass the Royal Pump Room Museum, then cross another zebra-crossing to the entrance of Valley Gardens. Enter

---

the gardens, then keep left on the lowest path, which runs beside a small stream. Follow this to the Magnesia Well Café and the area known as Bogs Field, which has an oval of flower beds around a fountain.

❹ From the far end of the oval take another path, through a ring of benches and then passing right of the tennis courts. Pass the start of a Link Trail to the Dales Way, then there's a mini-golf course on the left. Pass a bowling green on the right.

❺ In about 80yds (73m) the main path bends slightly left at the start of the Pinewoods. Take the path half-right, signed to Harlow Carr, alongside the Pinewoods map board. Follow the path through the woods to a road.

❻ Cross and go straight ahead through more woods and past an open area on the left. The path then runs along the edge of the wood, with fields and fine open views on the right. Pass a large binocular and panorama indicator. Continue straight ahead, descending now, to a road. Turn left and walk along to the entrance of Harlow Carr Gardens.

❼ Now you can retrace your steps back into Harrogate, or if you want to catch a bus back, keep on along the road past the car parks, to a main road. Turn left and the bus stop is about 100yds (91m) along on the left.

🍴 EATING AND DRINKING

Betty's tea room is a genteel Harrogate institution. Bettys was originally founded by a Swiss immigrant, and the Swiss influence is retained in much of the superb chocolate and patisserie on offer. Not only does the walk pass the main Betty's site near the beginning, but there's an offshoot at the end, beside the entrance to Harlow Carr. Of course, if Betty's should be packed out, Harrogate is bursting at the seams with pubs, coffee-shops and other eateries.

RICHMOND'S DRUMMER BOY

Following in the steps of the
Richmond Drummer to Easby Abbey.

The first part of the walk follows much of the route taken by the legendary
Richmond Drummer Boy. At the end of the 18th century, the story goes,
soldiers in Richmond Castle discovered a tunnel that was thought to lead
from there to Easby Abbey. They sent their drummer boy down it, beating
his drum so they could follow from above ground. His route went under the
Market Square and along to Frenchgate, then beside the river towards the
abbey. At the spot now marked by the Drummer Boy Stone, the drumming
stopped. The Drummer Boy was never seen again. The Green Howards
Regimental Museum in the Market Square can tell you more about the
drummer boy and his regiment.

Abbey and Church

The remnants of Easby Abbey are seen on this walk. It was founded for
Premonstratensian Canons in 1155 by the Constable of Richmond Castle.
Although little of the church remains, some of the other buildings survive
well, including the gatehouse, built about 1300. The refectory is also
impressive, and you can see the infirmary, the chapter house and the
dormitory. Just by the abbey ruins is the parish church, St Agatha's. It
contains a replica of the Anglo-Saxon Easby Cross (the original is in the British
Museum), and a set of medieval wall paintings showing Old Testament scenes
of Adam and Eve on the north wall, and the life of Jesus on the south, as well
as depictions of activities such as pruning and hawking.

After the abbey, you'll cross the River Swale on the old railway bridge,
and follow the track bed. This was part of the branch line from Richmond
to Darlington, which opened in 1846. It was closed in 1970. The station has
been restored as a cinema and shopping centre, with a café. Look right
over Richmond Bridge after you have passed below the castle to see how
the stonework differs from one end to the other. It was built by different
contractors, one working for Richmond Council and one for the North Riding
of Yorkshire. In the hillside below Billy Bank Wood, which you enter beyond
the bridge, were copper mines dating back to the 15th century.

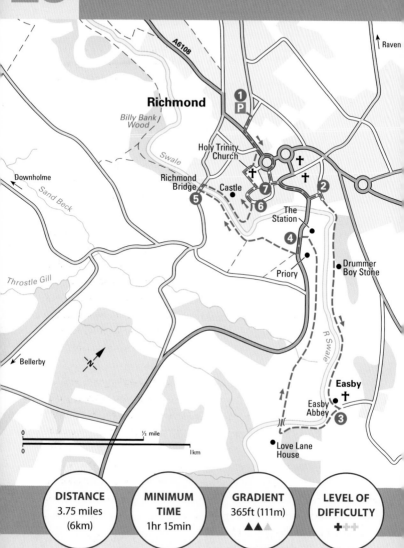

Raven

A6108

Richmond

Billy Bank Wood

Downholme

Sand Beck

Swale

Holy Trinity Church

Richmond Bridge

Castle

The Station

Priory

Drummer Boy Stone

Throstle Gill

R Swale

Bellerby

Easby

Easby Abbey

Love Lane House

N

0   ½ mile
0   1 km

DISTANCE	MINIMUM TIME	GRADIENT	LEVEL OF DIFFICULTY
3.75 miles (6km)	1hr 15min	365ft (111m) ▲▲▲	✛✛✛

PATHS Field and riverside paths, some town walking, no stiles
LANDSCAPE Valley of the River Swale and its steep banks
SUGGESTED MAP OS Explorer 304 Darlington & Richmond
START/FINISH Grid reference: NZ 168012
DOG FRIENDLINESS Dogs should be on lead for most of walk
PARKING Nuns Close long-stay car park
PUBLIC TOILETS Nuns Close car park, Richmond town centre and station

WALK 25 DIRECTIONS

❶ Leave the Nuns Close car park and turn right, then left at the T-junction. At the roundabout go on, down Ryder's Wynd. At the bottom turn left, then go right into Station Road. Just past the church, take Lombards Wynd left.

❷ Turn right at the next junction, along a lane which becomes a track. Follow the track, above the river, to a three-way fork. Take the middle path, which passes to the right of the Drummer Boy Stone. Follow this path to a gate into a field then bear right along the edge nearest the river, to a gate. Follow a track which runs beside the abbey in the village of Easby.

> **⛐ EATING AND DRINKING**
> The King's Head Hotel in the Market Square offers meals, sandwiches and afternoon teas. Seasons café in the station (go to the right of the building to find the entrance) is well known for its cakes.

❸ Just beyond the car park turn right, along another track. Follow the wall on the left to Love Lane House. Turn right over the old railway bridge. Follow the trackbed, crossing a metalled lane, to the station. Go to the left of the station building to the road.

❹ Turn left, up the road, then turn right up Priory Villas, and bear right to pass in front of the houses. From a gate walk between two sheds to another

gate, then along a clear path which gradually descends to run near the river. Walk beside a playing field and past the clubhouse to a road.

❺ Turn right to cross Richmond Bridge, then turn right along a riverside lane. Where the lane bends left by a car park, go to the river bank to see the Foss, then return to the lane.

❻ On a right-hand bend turn left up steps by the end of Castle Terrace, then turn right along a quiet cobbled street (sign for Richmond Castle) to emerge near the castle entrance. Walk down the street directly opposite the entrance, left of the market hall, to emerge into the market square.

❼ Turn left and walk to the town hall. Cross to Holy Trinity Church and continue ahead to the narrow entrance of Friars Wynd (sign for the Georgian Theatre Royal). At the end of the Wynd turn left to a zebra crossing, cross and continue along the road. Turn right up Hurgill Road to return to the car park.

> **⚘ IN THE AREA**
> Visit Richmond Castle, which looms over the Swale Valley. Its keep, more than 100ft (30m) high, was complete by 1180. Now in the care of English Heritage, the castle's central ward is surrounded by high curtain walls with towers. Inside the keep are drawings done in the First World War by conscientious objectors, who were imprisoned here.

TRAMPING FEWSTON'S SHORELINE

An easy stroll around a reservoir,
with plenty of wildlife to watch.

Fewston Reservoir was constructed in 1879 by the Leeds Waterworks Company and there's no doubt that the construction of these reservoirs transformed the secluded little valley. However, the passage of more than 130 years has softened the scars and the reservoirs are now treasured by many for their walking, wildlife and fishing possibilities.

For the angler, these reservoirs mostly mean one thing: trout. Wild brown trout are regularly caught at the northern end of Fewston Reservoir, where the river enters, and the lake is also kept stocked with rainbow trout from hatcheries. If you've got the gear and fancy a go yourself, permits can be bought from the little office by the car park entrance (when it's unmanned there's a ticket machine).

Wildlife to Watch For

With the fresh water, fringing forest and surrounding farmland, reservoirs like Fewston present a variety of wildlife habitats and there should always be something to see. The waters themselves are not particularly notable for waterfowl and waders, although the ubiquitous mallard, teal and tufted ducks are regular sights in winter. Geese are more obvious, with flocks of both Canada and greylag geese usually present, often grazing on fields alongside the path. Watch and listen for lapwings, too. This black and white bird, with its unmistakable crest, nests in damp meadows and often rises in agitated flight to lure intruders away from the nest. The forests are home to woodpeckers, tawny owls and sparrowhawks.

For much of the year, especially spring and early summer, Fewston Reservoir is a good place for wild flowers. Around the shoreline and in the damp meadows, look out for common valerian, common spotted orchid and cuckoo-flower. In late summer you can't miss the meadowsweet, with its frothy sprays of delicately-scented, creamy-white flowers – and only a very close look at the individual florets reveals any clues that this is a member of the rose family. The woods support a different range of species, including two that everyone can recognise: bluebells and wild garlic.

Opposite: View through the trees to Fewston Reservoir

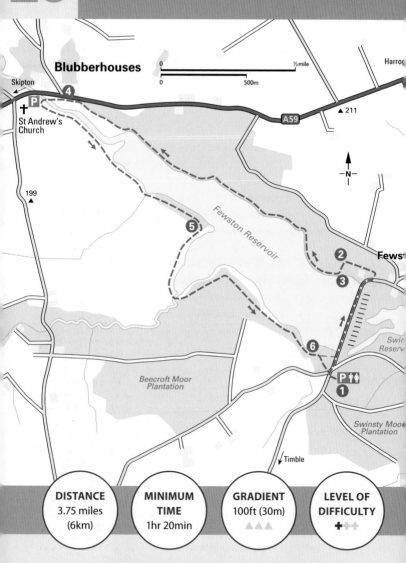

DISTANCE
3.75 miles
(6km)

MINIMUM
TIME
1hr 20min

GRADIENT
100ft (30m)
▲▲▲

LEVEL OF
DIFFICULTY
✚✚✚

PATHS Well made paths with some steps, no stiles
LANDSCAPE Woodland and waterside in a green valley
SUGGESTED MAP OS Explorer 297 Lower Wharfedale & Washburn Valley
START/FINISH Grid reference: SE 186537
DOG FRIENDLINESS Dogs can be off lead most of the way, but beware of geese
PARKING Swinsty Moor car cark
PUBLIC TOILETS Swinsty Moor car cark

WALK 26 DIRECTIONS

❶ Leave the car park and turn right to walk across the dam. At the end, near a Water Board house, follow the road round right and then go up steps on the left. Turn left at the top and follow a path near a wall above the house.

❷ Turn left again, down towards the reservoir, then turn right along a well-made path with a wall on the right and a wire fence on the left. Note the signs indicating that only anglers are allowed beyond the fence to the water's edge.

❸ Follow the path along near the water for about 1 mile (1.6km). It's not quite as flat as you might expect. Keep left at a fork to stay parallel to the water's edge. The reservoir narrows towards the far end and the path runs beside an area of growing vegetation which clearly hasn't been under water in some years. The busy A59 is in earshot before it comes into view.

❹ Go up steps to the main road, turn left along the pavement to cross a bridge, and then go down some more steps into a small car park. Turn left to a gate at the end and continue along another made path, which swings round into a substantial bay.

❺ Continue round the bay. Like the head of the reservoir, the bay is partly silted up, but don't be tempted to cut across, however low the water level may be, as the ground may not be as solid as it looks.

❻ Finally approaching the dam again, the path forks by a cluster of signs. Go right, up through a stand of tall pines, to emerge on the road opposite the car park entrance.

⊘ IN THE AREA

Head north into Nidderdale to visit Brimham Rocks, the weirdest of all Yorkshire's crags. They're made of the same millstone grit as many others, like nearby Guisecliff (see Walk 27), but at Brimham a unique combination of geology and the sand-blasting effect of the wind has sculpted dozens of free-standing towers and strangely-balanced boulders. The rocks s are open, and free, all year; the visitor centre, shop, and refreshment kiosk are open at weekends only in low season, and closed in January.

---

⑭ EATING AND DRINKING

In autumn you could feed a large family on blackberries gathered along the way, but failing this the obvious place to head for is the Timble Inn (turn sharp left out of the car park and you can't miss it). This Grade II listed former coaching inn was recently restored to create a crisp yet comfortable blend of old and new features. It serves meals from Wednesday to Sunday, using local produce freshly prepared and cooked with flair, and offers a selection of local ales.

CRAGS AND CREVASSES IN NIDDERDALE

Guisecliff's stark crags loom above lush woods,
while the moors provide vast prospects.

Nidderdale lies outside the Yorkshire Dales National Park but has the status of an Area of Outstanding Natural Beauty (AONB). One of the landscape features which earned the area such recognition is its ancient woodland, and Guisecliff Wood is one of the best examples. Today it's an enchanting environment of gnarled oak trees and moss-draped boulders.

Not all of the present wood has an unbroken history, as areas were cleared in the past to allow access for quarrying. Parts of Guise Cliff crag itself were quarried on a small scale, and there are several other disused quarries scattered around. There's little visible evidence of quarrying as you walk through the woods today, but soon after Guisecliff Tarn you join a level track across the hillside. In some places it's built up on a small embankment, while elsewhere it's incised into the slope. This track was clearly engineered to take heavy traffic such as laden carts.

After this, the walk makes a steep climb before emerging onto the moor near a radio mast; a much larger quarry lies just to the south. In the 19th century quarrying dominated this landscape. Much of the terraced housing in Pateley Bridge and Glasshouses was built for the quarrymen and their families. Stone was transported to Harrogate by a railway which reached Pateley Bridge in 1862. It closed to passengers in 1951 and to freight in 1964, but the boom years for the quarries were already long gone.

Grtistone Crag

Guise Cliff is the highest and most extensive gritstone crag in Yorkshire, reaching a height of almost 100ft (30m), and more than 120 climbing routes have been recorded. However, it is relatively unpopular compared to other crags in the area such as Brimham Rocks, Almscliff and Crookrise. This is largely due to its northerly aspect and the dense woods around its base, which together make the rocks lichenous and slow to dry.

Although the path runs quite close to the crags, you're hardly aware of the drop unless you venture out to the edge – but then it's sudden and absolute. If you have a head for heights, the edge offers terrific views over Nidderdale.

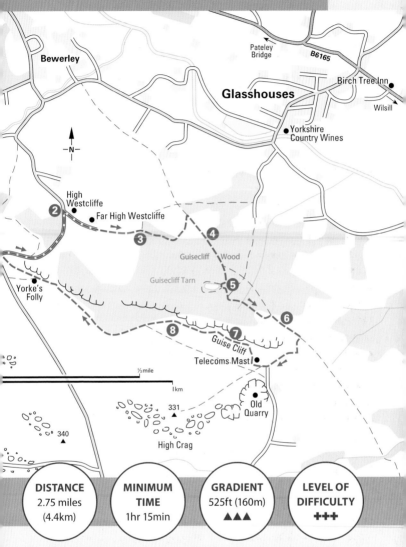

DISTANCE	MINIMUM TIME	GRADIENT	LEVEL OF DIFFICULTY
2.75 miles (4.4km)	1hr 15min	525ft (160m) ▲▲▲	+++

PATHS Field, woodland and moorland paths, generally clear, 2 stiles
LANDSCAPE Lush pastures and rocky woodlands below heather moors with a
fringe of crags **SUGGESTED MAP** OS Explorer 298 Nidderdale
START/FINISH Grid reference: SE 155636 **DOG FRIENDLINESS** Well-behaved
dogs can be off the lead in the woods **PARKING** Small parking area with
information board on sharp bend of Nought Bank Road **PUBLIC TOILETS** Pateley
Bridge **NOTE** Beware of 'crevasses' after Point ❻. The walk is safe if you stick to
the path, but small children and dogs should not be allowed to stray

WALK 27 DIRECTIONS

❶ Walk down the road. There are good verges at first, but take care lower down where the road narrows between walls. On a left-hand bend below the steepest section, turn right on a track opposite a footpath sign.

❷ Follow the track past High Westcliffe and Far High Westcliffe then out into a field. Go ahead to an old gatepost, and then bear left to a gate into woodland.

❸ Follow the track winding through the woods and out into another field. Stay with it till it bends left again, then turn sharp right along the lower edge of the field to another gate, with a gap-stile alongside, back into the woods.

❹ Follow the path ahead, between holly trees and on through the woods. Another path comes up from the left; keep ahead here, slightly uphill. The path curves right then forks. The right-hand fork goes towards large boulders; just beyond these is Guisecliff Tarn.

❺ Return to the fork and continue uphill. The path soon swings left and runs fairly level across the slope.

Approaching the edge of the woods, the path bears right up the hill.

❻ Climb the hill, keeping close to a wall on the left, towards a telecoms mast. Go through a gate left of the mast, ahead a few paces, then turn right along the enclosing fence. A sign here warns of dangerous crevasses, so take great care. Follow the fence round, then turn left alongside a wall. Go over a stile and continue. Before long you will see one of the crevasses on the left. The path continues to be safe enough but sometimes runs close to similar holes which are partly hidden by vegetation, especially in summer.

❼ The wall isn't continuous but the path is easy to follow. There are a few branches off to the right, which visit the edge of the crags. The views are impressive but the drops considerable.

❽ Continue until the path reaches moor on the left, beside a redundant stile. Continue along the path, following the wall then cutting off a corner to a gate near Yorke's Folly. Pass just right of the folly and follow the path downhill back to the start.

🍴 EATING AND DRINKING

There's a wide choice in Pateley Bridge, but the closest place is the tea room at Yorkshire Country Wines in Glasshouses. This is open Wednesday–Sunday from Easter to October, weekends only the rest of the year. On the B6165 between Glasshouses and Wilsill you'll find the friendly Birch Tree Inn, serving local beers and offering an extensive menu.

REETH AND MAIDEN CASTLE

From Reeth's village green, a path crosses
the Swale and climbs to an ancient hillfort.

Reeth, the 'capital' of Swaledale, is first recorded in Saxon times, but the area
has been populated for much longer, and this walk explores several aspects
of its prehistory, including an ancient hil-lfort.

Prehistoric Swaledale

After crossing the Swale, the walk climbs through fields and onto open moor
to reach Maiden Castle. This is usually described as Iron Age (after 750 BC), but
there are no archaeological finds to confirm the date. However, it is similar in
its layout to other hill-forts for which the Iron Age evidence is stronger.

Some authorities have questioned whether it is a fort, arguing that the
rising slope directly to the south would weaken its defensive value. They
suggest instead that it was primarily a ritual or religious site. One piece of
evidence that may support this view is the long avenue, bounded by stones,
leading into the main enclosure. Even today it has a ceremonial feel as you
walk down the avenue to enter the main, roughly oval, enclosure with its
impressive ditch and outer rampart. As no one really knows what it was
for, you can let your imagination run free. One thing that is certain is that it
commands a magnificent view over Swaledale.

On the way up to Maiden Castle you will pass the remains of a small round
barrow (or bowl barrow), a burial mound probably of Bronze Age (before 750
BC) or even Neolithic origin.

The Power of the Flood

After descending from Maiden Castle, you return along the banks of
the Swale. Though usually placid, this reach of the river can flood with
exceptional speed: a rise of 10ft (3m) in 20 minutes has been observed. One
factor may be the large areas of bare ground on the fellsides, a legacy of
lead-mining days, which shed rainfall directly into the becks and rivers. Just
downstream of the swingbridge, floods have left an extensive area of bare
stones and gravel, and the bridge itself is also a memorial to their power. Its
predecessor, built in 1920, was destroyed by a flood in 2000.

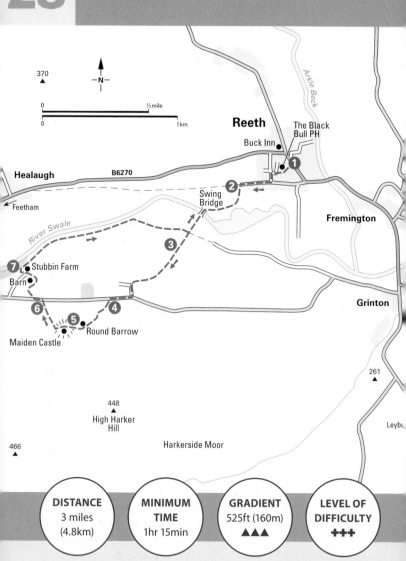

370 ▲

→N←

0 ────────── ½ mile
0 ────────── 1 km

Reeth

The Black Bull PH

Buck Inn •

Healaugh

B6270

❶

Feetham →

Swing Bridge

❷

← ←

River Swale

Fremington

❸

❼
• Stubbin Farm

Barn •

❹

Grinton

❻

❺
• Round Barrow

Maiden Castle

261 ▲

Leyb[

448 ▲
High Harker Hill

466 ▲

Harkerside Moor

DISTANCE	MINIMUM TIME	GRADIENT	LEVEL OF DIFFICULTY
3 miles (4.8km)	1hr 15min	525ft (160m) ▲▲▲	+++

PATHS Tracks, moorland and farmland paths, sometimes indistinct through fields, 1 stile **LANDSCAPE** Riverside, farmland and elevated heather moorland
SUGGESTED MAP OS Explorer OL30 Yorkshire Dales: North & Central
START/FINISH Grid reference: SE 037992
DOG FRIENDLINESS Few opportunities for dogs to roam free
PARKING Around the green in Reeth (honesty box)
PUBLIC TOILETS At upper end of green in Reeth

WALK 28 DIRECTIONS

❶ Leave the green at its south-west corner, passing the National Park Centre, and walk into Anvil Square. Bear right, past the Garden House, into a narrow, walled path signed 'To the River'. Continue along a lane to a T-junction. Turn left and at the next junction turn right (signed 'Doctor's Surgery'). After the medical centre the lane soon turns to a stony track with a flagged path alongside. Where the track ends turn left down a narrower stony path.

❷ At the bottom go through a gate and bear right on a boardwalk. Continue through fields to the swingbridge. Cross the bridge and continue almost straight ahead, following the sign to Harkerside. Go over a plank bridge (usually redundant), then continue left of a clump of trees and up to a small stile.

> ⑪ **EATING AND DRINKING**
> There are several cafés and pubs around the green in Reeth. Try The Black Bull, with its glass-fronted dining room and outside tables, which serves serves hand-pumped ale and good food.

❸ Follow the direction of another fingerpost to a gate and continue up to meet a clear track as it goes through a gateway. Turn right along the track to farmyard, then turn left up the access track to a lane and turn right.

❹ Where the wall on the left ends, go up through rushes to find a small path going diagonally up the slope towards a green knoll. From the knoll (the round barrow) you can see two parallel lines of stones, like collapsed walls, running through the heather. Follow a thin path between these to the bank and ditch enclosing Maiden Castle.

❺ The path continues across the centre of the fort, but the best option is probably to follow the right-hand edge, above the ditch. At the far end, just below a tree, a path crosses the ditch. Follow this, heading diagonally downhill to meet the lane again at its junction with another track.

❻ Go left along the lane, then follow the wall on the right downhill through rushes and ferns to a gate just right of a small barn. Go down the field, first right then back left to a gate into a farmyard. Go through a series of gates left of the farmhouse and its attached barn, and down a short walled track.

❼ Turn right along a green terrace above the river until a small path slants down to a gate on the river bank. Follow the riverside path for about 0.5 miles (800m) until the river curves away left. Bear slightly right on a green track to a gate, then along the edge of a field until directly opposite the swingbridge. Turn left to the bridge, cross and retrace the first stage of the walk back into Reeth.

VILLAGES, FALLS AND INTRIGUING FOLLIES

From West Burton to Aysgarth and back, via the famous
Aysgarth Falls and some unusual farm buildings.

Many people regard West Burton as the prettiest village in the Dales. Its
wide, irregular green, with a fat obelisk of 1820, is surrounded by small stone
cottages, formerly homes to the quarrymen and miners of the district – but
no church. At the end of the walk you'll travel for a short time, near Flanders
Hall, along Morpeth Gate, the old packhorse route to Middleham.

After crossing the wide flood plain of Bishopdale Beck, and crossing
Eshington Bridge, you climb across the hill to descend into Aysgarth. The walk
takes you along the traditional field path from one part of the village to its
other half, set around St Andrew's Church. It's worth looking inside; it contains
the spectacular choir screen brought here from Jervaulx Abbey, carved by the
renowned Ripon workshops.

The Falls and the Wood

Beyond the church, the path follows the river beside Aysgarth's Middle and
Lower Falls. The falls were formed by the Ure eating away at the underlying
limestone as it descends from Upper Wensleydale to join the deeper
Bishopdale. They are now one of the most popular tourist sights in the
Yorkshire Dales National Park and the Upper Falls, by the bridge, featured in
the film *Robin Hood, Prince of Thieves*. Robin (Kevin Costner) and Little John
fought here with long staves.

Mrs Sykes' Follies

On the return leg of the walk, you pass below two oddities in the parkland
behind the house at Sorrellsykes Park. These two follies were built in the 18th
century by Mrs Sykes and no one seems to knows why. One is a round tower,
with a narrowing waist like a diabolo. The other, sitting like Thunderbird
3 ready for lift-off, is known to local people as the 'Rocket Ship'. It is of no
practical use, except for minimal shelter in the square room in its base, but
it is just one of many folly cones throughout Britain. None of the others,
however, have this elaborate arrangement of fins – presumably added
because the builder had doubts about its stability.

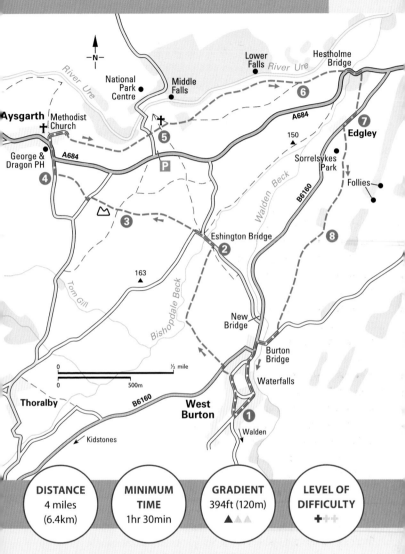

DISTANCE	MINIMUM TIME	GRADIENT	LEVEL OF DIFFICULTY
4 miles (6.4km)	1hr 30min	394ft (120m) ▲▲△△	✚✚✚

PATHS Field and riverside paths and tracks, 35 stiles
LANDSCAPE Two typical Dales villages, fields and falls on the River Ure
SUGGESTED MAP OS Explorer OL30 Yorkshire Dales: Northern & Central
START/FINISH Grid reference: SE 017867
DOG FRIENDLINESS Dogs should be on lead
PARKING Centre of West Burton, by (but not on) the Green
PUBLIC TOILETS None en route; Aysgarth National Park Centre is close

WALK 29 DIRECTIONS

❶ Leave the Green near the Village Shop. Opposite 'Meadowcroft' go left, signed 'Eshington Bridge'. Cross the road, turn right then left, through a gate and down steps. Go through a gate beside a barn, and continue to a stile at the bottom right of the field. Cross two more stiles then bear right to meet a stone wall. Follow this then continue ahead to a road.

❷ Turn left, cross the bridge and go up a lane to a bend. Go ahead through a stile, signed 'Aysgarth'. Climb past a stile and left of a barn. Continue up the field and bear left to a gate near the corner, then diagonally across the next field. Keep left of an obvious wall gap to a stile by another gap. Descend to a stile and footpath sign.

❸ Continue in the same direction and up to a signpost. Follow the Aysgarth direction to a gateway and stile. Cross the field half left to a stile on to a lane. Turn left, then right, signed 'Aysgarth'. Go through three stiles to a road.

❹ Turn right, into the village. Go past the George and Dragon then ahead to the Methodist Church and bear right along the lane. Cross a stile by Field House. Follow the wall and continue along a short track, then follow a path through eight stiles to a road.

❺ Enter the churchyard, pass right of the church and leave by a stile. Cross

> 🍴 **EATING AND DRINKING**
> In Aysgarth, the George and Dragon is a good family pub serving meals. Up the road from the church, just off the walk route, Palmer Flatt Hotel has bar meals, a restaurant and a beer garden. In West Burton, the Fox and Hounds is a traditional village pub serving meals. Aysgarth Falls National Park Centre, across the river from the church, has a good coffee shop.

a field and go through a wood. Follow the path downhill, descending steps to the river bank. Take a signed stile right.

❻ Follow the path by the river to a signpost. Bend right across a field to the main road. Turn left, cross a bridge, then turn right into woodland, signed 'Edgley', soon bearing left, uphill, to a stile. Bear right across a field to a gate in the far corner and join a road.

❼ Turn right. About 150yds (137m) along, go left over a stile, signed 'Flanders Hall'. Walk towards the follies, then bear right just below the ridge, passing Sorrelsykes Park to your right. Cross a track and bear left past a waymark to a signpost. Turn right to a stepped stone stile, then follow the bottom edge of the field to a gate opposite a stone barn.

❽ Descend through this and two gates, then bear left along the field-edge to a stile. Continue to a lane. Turn right, cross a bridge and join the village road. Turn left, back to the Green.

Opposite: The village of West Burton

GRASSINGTON AND LINTON FALLS

Exploring a picturesque village, with stepping-stones and a historic church along the way.

Grassington today may appear a peaceful place, but its history is turbulent and industrial. The moors to the north and east were an important area for lead mining from the 15th century onwards. The industry developed rapidly in the later 18th and early 19th centuries. An influx of mine-workers created a rough, 'boom-town' atmosphere. The lead-mining industry declined in the last quarter of the 19th century, but the opening of a railway to Skipton in 1901 brought a new influx of more pacific visitors, and tourism has been a mainstay of Grassington ever since.

Falls and Stepping-stones

Linton Falls funnel most of the water of the River Wharfe through a narrow channel. The falls are not as spectacular as others in the area, but their rocky setting is appealing, and they can be impressive when the river is high.

When the river is high, the stepping-stones at Point ❹ can become impassable. Given more normal water levels (and no ice), they are quite safe, at least for normally agile adults. However the gaps between stones may be too wide for smaller children to manage easily. An alternative, at least in summer, is to paddle across. The best place to do this is a few paces upstream of the stones, as the current speeds up where it funnels between them. If in doubt, the safest course is to backtrack to the bridge by Linton Falls.

St Michael and All Angels

Once the stepping-stones would have been used by parishioners in their Sunday best heading for the church, which for centuries served Grassington as well as Linton. Its isolated position is probably explained by being sited over a former pagan place of worship. There was almost certainly a church here in Saxon times, but the origins of the present building are Norman, and it has been extended and altered many times since. There are many features inside and out, including a rare survival of a church chest, used to store valuables such as vestments and relics. This had five keys, kept separately by the priest and four church wardens – security concerns are nothing new.

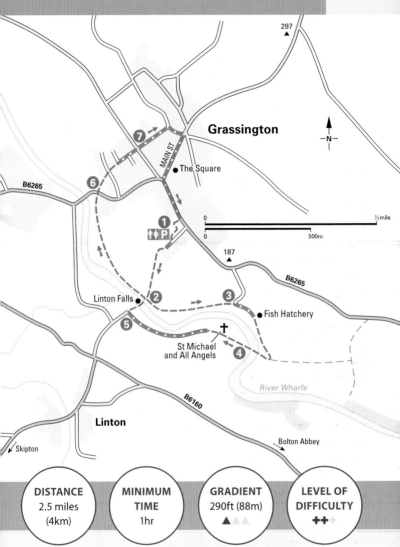

DISTANCE	MINIMUM TIME	GRADIENT	LEVEL OF DIFFICULTY
2.5 miles (4km)	1hr	290ft (88m) ▲▲△	++

PATHS Mix of pavement, lanes and field paths, stepping-stones across a river, 2 stiles **LANDSCAPE** Historic villages and gentle riverside scenery
SUGGESTED MAP OS Explorer OL2 Yorkshire Dales: South & West
START/FINISH Grid reference: SE 002637 **DOG FRIENDLINESS** Mostly on lead, but may be able to run free when there's no stock in the riverside fields
PARKING National Park Centre car park, Grassington **PUBLIC TOILETS** National Park Centre car park, Grassington; also near Linton church

WALK 30 DIRECTIONS

❶ Walk down through the car park to the bottom left corner, where there's a gate onto a narrow path. Continue down this path to a footbridge over the River Wharfe. This is Linton Falls.

❷ Don't cross the bridge now – you'll come back this way later. Instead turn left (signed to Hebden and Burnsall) and follow a well-worn path through a narrow gap-stile and then another stile with a little gate. Continue along the path, which climbs above the river, to reach steps and a gated stile into a lane.

❸ Turn right down the lane and follow it past houses and a fish-hatchery. The lane becomes a gravel track. Go through a gate and bear right to a line of stepping-stones across the river.

❹ Having crossed the stepping-stones, continue straight ahead to a gate at the corner of Linton churchyard. Walk through the churchyard and out to a lane. Follow the lane past several rows of cottages until a footpath sign points down right to Linton Falls.

✐ IN THE AREA

Grassington is about 9 miles (14.5km) from Bolton Abbey. Apart from the beautiful ruins of the 12th-century priory, the Abbey Estate has many fine walks. There are also the Hesketh Farm Park, two gift shops, several cafés and restaurants.

🍴 EATING AND DRINKING

Grassington has a good choice of cafés and pubs. One place that stands out is 5 The Square, the restaurant of Grassington House Hotel, which has an elegant dining room and relaxed bar serving contemporary food based around fresh local ingredients. Try griddled Thirsk rare breed cured pork with pineapple, for example.

---

❺ Go down steps and along a narrow walled path to the footbridge and cross it, directly above the falls, to return to Point **❷**. It's possible to go ahead for a quick return to the car park, but instead turn left (sign for Grass Wood) and follow another well-trodden path near the river and across a field to meet a road (B6265) just above a bridge.

❻ Go straight across, ahead a few paces, then turn right up a footpath (sign for Wood Lane). Follow this path up to a street. Go straight across, up some steps and follow the path round and up to another street. Follow the road straight ahead and up to a crossroads. Go straight across into Moody Sty Lane.

❼ Walk up about 250yds (229m) then turn right into Garrs End Lane. Follow this to its end and turn right (Main Street). Follow this down to the Square (really more of a triangle) at the centre of Grassington. Continue down a few more paces and turn left on the B6265 to return to the main car park.

EMBSAY'S MINI MOUNTAIN

A steep climb leads up to a rocky summit
with far-reaching views.

Barden Moor is a broad swathe of heather moorland, largely managed
for grouse and also valued as a water catchment area. As well as the small
Embsay Reservoir there are two larger reservoirs on the moor. Owned by the
Bolton Abbey Estate, the moor has been open for public access since 1968.
Its fringe of gritstone crags is popular with rockclimbers, while its wide open
spaces offer some tough but rewarding walks, and the main bridleway (not
the one used on this walk) is an excellent mountain bike route. The climb to
Embsay Crag, though steep in places, is one of the easiest ways to get a taste
of this expanse. The Crag's rocky summit is attractive in itself and offers a
great view, not only over the southern flanks of the moor but extending far
and wide. The rooftops of Skipton, the sweep of the Ribble Valley and the
distinctive outline of Pendle Hill all compete for attention.

Embsay Mills

In the early stages of the Industrial Revolution there were six water-driven
spinning and weaving mills in Embsay and Eastby. The development of the
Leeds and Liverpool Canal (finally completed in 1816) encouraged a shift
to larger mills in nearby Skipton, and this was reinforced by the arrival of
railways. Embsay Station opened in 1888 as part of the Midland Railway
branch-line between Skipton and Ilkley. The station is now Embsay's main
attraction as part of a heritage railway.

Several mills remain, though mostly turned to other uses – for instance, one
is now a large needlecraft centre. The walk passes a millpond which was used
to control the water supply to this and other mills. Higher up the track to the
reservoir you'll also spot a mill chimney: this was the Crown Spindle Mill.

Sails and Trout

Embsay Reservoir is more recent, being constructed in the early 20th century.
At time of writing there is extensive work going on to replace the overflow
spillway (due for completion in 2011). The reservoir is also home to Craven
Sailing Club and is used for fly-fishing.

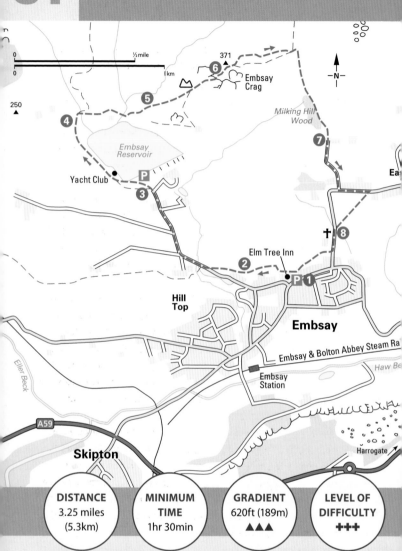

DISTANCE	MINIMUM TIME	GRADIENT	LEVEL OF DIFFICULTY
3.25 miles (5.3km)	1hr 30min	620ft (189m) ▲▲▲	+++

PATHS Fields, lanes and tracks leading to some steep rough paths on the heights, 9 stiles **LANDSCAPE** Heather moors and gritstone crags above green pastures and villages **SUGGESTED MAP** OS Explorer OL2 Yorkshire Dales: South & West **START/FINISH** Grid reference: SE 009538 **DOG FRIENDLINESS** Under the terms of the Barden Moor Access Agreement, dogs are allowed only on rights of way **PARKING** Free car park in Embsay, near Elm Tree Inn **PUBLIC TOILETS** None on route **NOTE** Parts of Barden Moor may be closed during the shooting season (August and September) or when there is high fire risk

WALK 31 DIRECTIONS

1 Go through a gate at the back of the car park, and bear left to a stile in the far corner of the field. Bear right a bit to a gate in a hedge, then walk along just above school grounds. Continue along the fence to a stile in a stone wall, and cross a track to a stile in a fence. Cross a field (look out for horses) to a stile.

2 Bear slightly right, go round the curve of a hedge and find another stile at the angle of two walls. Go straight ahead to a stile beside a gate, and ahead again to a stile and steps down to a lane, with a millpond on the far side. Turn right up the lane and follow it for about 700yds (640m), through a right-hand bend to a left-hand bend below the reservoir car park.

3 Here the lane becomes a track. Follow it up to the level of the dam, past the yacht club and beside the reservoir, then up slightly to a gateway where it emerges onto open moorland.

4 Go ahead a few paces. Then, as the track starts to curve left, turn right on a smaller track (bridleway sign). Follow this for 250yds (229m), then fork right towards the reservoir wall near some trees. Dip down to cross a bridge, then follow the path, soon moving away from the wall again. There are blue-topped marker posts; these can disappear when the bracken is high, but the path itself is always clear. Embsay Crag rises steeply ahead.

5 Keep straight on up the main path as it climbs more steeply onto the upper slopes. The final stretch is very steep. Finally emerge onto the summit.

6 Continue on the path to gradually descend and bear right to meet a wall. Turn right through a gate by a signpost (footpath and bridleway to Eastby). Walk down a field, with a wall on your right, to the top of a wood then down the track along its left-hand side. Near a farm-cum-4x4-dealer, meet a tarmac track and continue ahead on it.

7 Emerge onto a road. Turn left and walk with care (narrow verges), with houses on the left, for 250yds (229m). Shortly before the first house on the right, turn right onto a footpath. This soon bears right to cross two fields and meet the road near Embsay church.

8 Cross, turn left and walk down the pavement to a gate and footpath sign by the entrance to a house. Cross the field diagonally to the far corner and a stile. Follow a path to a stile, then down the field to the gate into the car park.

> **🍴 EATING AND DRINKING**
> Right next to the car park, the Elm Tree Inn is a popular, friendly and unpretentious village pub. There's a blazing fire in the winter, and the menu offers few surprises but is well prepared and reasonably priced. You'll also find a good selection of real ales, mostly from local breweries.

CONISTONE DIB

Ascend a hidden gorge onto the moors,
before an easy descent with great views.

Unlike Kilnsey Crag, which practically punches you in the face as you
travel along this section of Wharfedale, the gorge of Conistone Dib is
easily overlooked. The lower part in particular, known as Gurling Trough,
is particularly well hidden. Above it the valley opens out before narrowing
again into another little gorge.

Marks of the Ice Age

The origin of these landscape features is believed to lie at the end of the last
ice age, when glaciers still filled some of the valleys and covered most of the
uplands. Torrents of meltwater scoured many channels which today are often
dry. Some channels may even have been formed underneath the ice, where
the water may have been under pressure, flowing in a virtual pipe (and as a
result could even flow uphill). Waterfalls plunged over bands of harder rock,
wearing away at softer rocks beneath until the lip collapsed, causing the fall
to retreat. (The grandest example of this is a few miles away at Malham Cove.)

There are many other ice age relics to be seen on this walk. The descent
brings a view down to Kilnsey Crag, where a spur of rock was effectively sliced
off by the glacier grinding past. The overhanging rocks of Kilnsey are even
more striking because they overlook a conspicuously level area of the valley
floor. This stretches from well below Conistone Bridge up to the meeting
of the Wharfe and the River Skirfare coming from Littondale, a distance of
around 1.25 miles (2km). This land was once a lake, formed behind a natural
dam or moraine deposited by a shrinking glacier. Gradually the rivers washed
down enough silt to fill up the lake and today it's green and fertile, though
occasionally subject to flooding.

Above Gurling Trough is a level, dry valley, before the path forks. The
described route goes right, but you can keep straight ahead into another
section of rocky gorge. You should be aware that this direct route involves a
bit of scrambling at its head. It shouldn't be much bother to an agile adult and
most children will love it, but it is very significantly harder than anything else
on the walk. The described route avoids it, coming back in just above.

Kettlewell

River Wharfe

B6160

Tennant Arms PH

Kilnsey

St Mary's Church ✝

Conistone

SCOT GATE LANE

Trough

Gurling

Dib

330 ▲

Grassington

DISTANCE	MINIMUM TIME	GRADIENT	LEVEL OF DIFFICULTY
2.25 miles (3.6km)	1hr	510ft (155m) ▲▲▲	+++

PATHS Mostly easy grassy paths and good tracks, but a few short rocky sections; no stiles **LANDSCAPE** A secluded gorge leads onto open moorland
SUGGESTED MAP OS Explorer OL2 Yorkshire Dales: South & West
START/FINISH Grid reference: SD 979674
DOG FRIENDLINESS The walled sections of Scot Gate Lane offer the best chance for dogs to run free **PARKING** Limited in village; better to park on verges by Conistone Bridge **PUBLIC TOILETS** None on route

WALK 32 DIRECTIONS

1 Walk up the road from the bridge into the village. Keep left past a triangular enclosure in the centre of the village. The lane swings left (sign for St Mary's Church). Immediately go right on a stony track across a green. Keep right where the track forks, and walk up to a gate and footpath sign.

2 Continue up the track, which soon becomes grassy and then rough and rocky as it enters the narrowing valley of Gurling Trough. Follow the path, with a few rocky steps, up the bed of the little gorge, then emerge into a more open valley. Continue up the green track in the valley bed, pass through a gate and enjoy easy, level walking for about 300yds (274m).

3 Where the path forks, bear right. Go through a gate and follow a path up a shallow side valley. As it emerges onto open ground, turn left on a small sheep track. Meet an obvious track and turn left again. (If you miss the sheep track don't worry, as you'll meet the obvious track anyway, just before a wall.) Follow the track to overlook the head of the rocky gorge, where the direct route emerges.

4 Continue between walls to a gate and signpost. Bear left, meet a clear stony track and follow it downhill. Continue down this track (Scot Gate Lane), past a mobile phone tower, with views over Wharfedale and Littondale. The grey thrust of Kilnsey Crag becomes obvious ahead, low down on the opposite slope.

5 Where the track meets a lane, turn left and walk past the little Church of St Mary back into Conistone village. Turn right to return to the bridge.

🔎 IN THE AREA

Take a closer look at Kilnsey Crag (but do not park on the road directly below). It's an impressive sight with its leaning walls and jutting main overhang, and has long been a draw to climbers, for whom it ranks as one of the major crags of the Dales. The lip of the overhang is about 40ft (12m) out from the base. It was finally climbed 'free' (using ropes only for protection, not for direct aid) by Mark Leach in 1988. He named the route 'Mandela' because most people had thought it would never go free.

🍴 EATING AND DRINKING

The Tennant Arms sits almost directly beneath the thrust of Kilnsey Crag and is perennially popular with climbers as well as walkers. There is a choice of hand-pumped Yorkshire ales. The menu relies on local suppliers and everything is cooked freshly to order. Muddy boots are no problem in the bar, but walkers are requested not to wear them in carpeted areas.

Opposite: View from below Kilnsey Crag

ALONG THE CANAL AT GARGRAVE

Following the Leeds and
Liverpool Canal from Gargrave.

Gargrave has long been a stopping-off point for travellers from the cities of West Yorkshire on their way to the coast at Morecambe or to the Lake District. These days, most of them arrive along the A65 from Skipton, the route formerly taken by horse-drawn coaches. Its position also proved important when 18th- and 19th-century surveyors were seeking westward routes for other methods of transport. The walk crosses the railway not long after leaving Gargrave; this is the route that, not far west, becomes the Settle-to-Carlisle line. You return to the village beside the Leeds and Liverpool Canal.

Earlier Settlers, Mills and Bandages

Although Gargrave is today mostly a 19th-century settlement, there is evidence that the area has been in occupation much longer. The site of a Roman villa has been identified near by, while on West Street, excavation has found the remains of a moated homestead dating from the 13th century, with a smithy and a lime pit, that was reused in the 15th century. By the 18th century, there were cotton mills in Gargrave, served by the canal, and weavers were engaged in producing cloth for the clothing industry. Their expertise resulted in the establishment here of one of the village's biggest employers, Johnson & Johnson Medical, where they found workers who could undertake the fine weaving that was needed to produce their bandages.

Canal Digging

It wasn't until 1810 that the canal crossed the Pennines, and barges could go from Leeds to Blackburn, and 1816 before barges could reach Liverpool. Gargrave benefited not only from the access it gave the village to the raw materials for the cotton mills, but also as a stopping place for the bargees.

    The walk joins the canal near the lowest of the six locks at Bank Newton, where the canal begins a serpentine course to gain height as it starts its trans-Pennine journey. Near the lock is the former canal company boatyard where boats for maintaining the canal were built. Along the tow path, you will cross the Priest Holme Aqueduct, where the canal is carried over the River Aire.

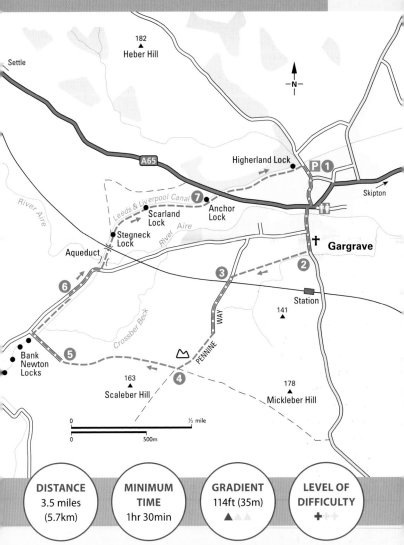

DISTANCE	MINIMUM TIME	GRADIENT	LEVEL OF DIFFICULTY
3.5 miles (5.7km)	1hr 30min	114ft (35m) ▲▲▲	✚✚✚

PATHS Field paths and tracks, then canal tow path, 1 stile

LANDSCAPE Farmland and canal side

SUGGESTED MAP OS Explorer OL2 Yorkshire Dales: Southern & Western

START/FINISH Grid reference: SD 931539

DOG FRIENDLINESS Dogs should be on lead, except on the canal bank

PARKING Car park near Village Hall, signed from A65

PUBLIC TOILETS By bridge in Gargrave

WALK 33 DIRECTIONS

❶ Walk down the lane, past Gargrave Village Hall. At the main road turn right, cross the road and go left into Church Street and over the bridge. Pass the church on your left. Just past Church Close House on your right, turn right, following a Pennine Way sign. Go over a stone stile in the wall on your left.

❷ Turn right along the wall, following the Pennine Way path, which is partly paved here. Go ahead across the field to a waymarked gate, then half left to another gate. Walk up the field, left of power lines, to a gate that leads to a rough sunken lane.

❸ Turn left, over a railway bridge, then follow the track up a small hill. Cross a cattle grid, then leave the track to cross a stile on the left into a field. Take a faint path half right then join a track, making for a signpost on the skyline.

❹ At the post, turn right to the corner of a wire fence, then slant down a grassy ramp to reach a waymarked gate in a crossing fence. Go ahead

🍴 EATING AND DRINKING

Gargrave has several restaurants, tea shops and cafés. The Dalesman Café and Sweet Emporium, to give it its full name, is a Dales institution especially popular with cyclists. The Bridge Restaurant is also recommended. The Old Swan Inn on the A65 has meals at lunchtimes and in the evenings.

⌖ IN THE AREA

Explore more canal history at nearby Skipton, where the Leeds and Liverpool Canal runs through the heart of the old town. You should also visit the fine parish church at the top of the High Street, and the nearby castle, with its splendid twin-towered gatehouse. Conduit Court, the heart of the castle, has a fine old yew tree in its centre.

across the field to a pair of gates. Take the waymarked left-hand one and continue ahead, at first following a fence and line of trees. Continue to meet a track and turn right.

❺ Follow the track down to the canal by Bank Newton Locks. Cross the bridge and turn right along the tow path. Where the tow path runs out, join the lane alongside the canal.

❻ Go ahead along the lane, cross the bridge over the canal then turn right down a spiral path to go under the bridge and continue along the tow path. Pass over a small aqueduct over the river, then under a railway bridge. Continue past Stegneck Lock and Scarland Lock to reach Anchor Lock.

❼ Beyond the lock, opposite the Anchor Inn, go under the road bridge and along the tow path to reach Bridge 170, at Higherland Lock. Go on to the road by a signpost. Turn right down the road, back to the car park.

LEGENDARY SEMER WATER

Discover the tall tales which surround
Yorkshire's biggest natural lake.

Semer Water was formed at the end of the last ice age. Glacial meltwater attempted to drain away down the valley which the glacier had gouged out of the limestone. It was prevented from doing so by a wall of boulder clay, dumped by the glacier itself, across the valley's end. So the water built up, forming an enormous lake which once stretched 3 miles (4.8km) up Raydale. Natural silting has gradually filled the upper part of the lake bed, leaving Semer Water – at 0.5 miles (800m) long, North Yorkshire's largest natural lake.

Legends of the Lake

Semer Water boasts several legends. One concerns the three huge blocks of limestone deposited by the departing glacier at the water's edge at the north end of the lake. Named the Carlow Stone and the Mermaid Stones, they are said to have landed here when the Devil and a giant who lived on Addlebrough, the prominent hill 1 mile (1.6km) to the east, began lobbing missiles at each other.

More famous is the story of the beggar who came to the town that once stood where the lake is now. He went from door to door, asking for food and drink, but was refused by everyone – except the poorest couple. Revealing himself as an angel, he raised his staff over the town, crying 'Semer Water rise, Semer Water sink, And swallow all save this little house, That gave me meat and drink.' The waters overwhelmed the town, leaving the poor people's cottage on the brink of the new lake. Some say the church bells can still be heard ringing beneath the waters.

Behind the Legend

There are indeed the remains of a settlement beneath Semer Water. Houses perched on stilts were built along the water's edge in Iron Age times, though there may have been an earlier settlement here in neolithic times, too, for flint arrow heads have been found. A Bronze Age spear head was found in 1937 when the lake's waters were lowered.

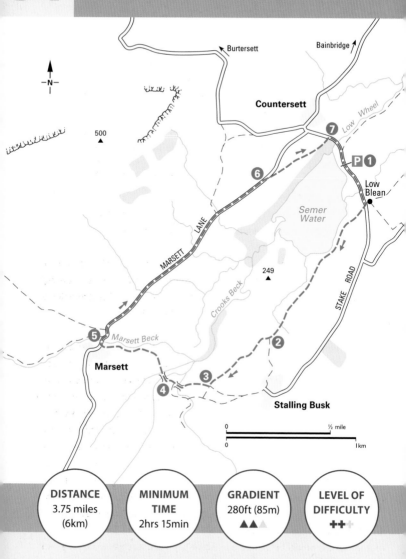

DISTANCE
3.75 miles
(6km)

MINIMUM
TIME
2hrs 15min

GRADIENT
280ft (85m)
▲▲▲

LEVEL OF
DIFFICULTY
+++

PATHS Field paths and tracks, can be damp in places, 12 stiles
LANDSCAPE Valley, lake and scattered woodland
SUGGESTED MAP OS Explorer OL30 Yorkshire Dales: Northern & Central
START/FINISH Grid reference: SD 921875
DOG FRIENDLINESS Dogs should be on lead
PARKING Car park at the north end of the lake, pay at nearby Low Blean Farm
PUBLIC TOILETS None on route

WALK 34 DIRECTIONS

❶ Turn right from the car park up the road. Opposite Low Blean farm, go right over a stile, signed 'Stalling Busk'. Cross a stile and head toward a barn. Pass right of it to find a clearer path. Follow this to pass a Wildlife Trust sign. Continue past an information board then skirt above an old graveyard to a gate and signpost just beyond.

❷ Follow the Marsett sign into the field corner and cross a gated stile. Follow the level path through more stiles, then across a larger field, keeping just above a steeper slope. Pass right of a barn among trees, then cross a stream bed.

❸ Bear right immediately on a narrow path, descending gently above a roofless barn to a stile. Continue to a stile at the corner of another barn, then turn right immediately across a level meadow, with a wall on your right. Cross the wall at a gate, then follow it to a footbridge. Cross and go straight ahead to another footbridge beside a ford.

❹ Continue along the track, meeting another river. Approaching Marsett, bear right across a green, following the

> **⊘ IN THE AREA**
> Visit Bainbridge, with its wide green and attractive houses. The Romans had a fort here, Virosidum, on top of the hill called Brough. The River Bain, crossed by the bridge which gives the village its name, is England's shortest river, running all of 2 miles (3.2km) from Semer Water to the River Ure.

stream, to a red telephone box. Turn right over the bridge.

❺ Continue along the lane for about 0.75 miles (1.2km) to a stile on the right with a yellow-topped post and sign to Semer Water Bridge.

❻ Descend to a yellow-topped post and continue to a post by a gate. Go through and follow the wall on the left to a ford (usually shallow), with another fingerpost just beyond. Follow the direction of the finger as the track is a bit vague here, becoming clearer again as it descends to cross a damp patch and runs n into trees. The lake is about 30yds (27m) away on the right. Follow the path to a gate onto the road.

❼ Turn right and follow the lane over the bridge and back to the car park.

> **⊛ EATING AND DRINKING**
> The nearest place to Semer Water is Bainbridge, where the Rose and Crown Hotel by the Green dates back more than 500 years. The Bainbridge Horn, blown to guide travellers to the village in the dark winter months, hangs here. The hotel serves home-cooked local produce both in the bars and, in the evening, in the Dales Room Restaurant.

HALTON GILL AND FOXUP

Enjoy a walk through classic scenery
deep in the Dales.

There are no summits on this walk, no great crags, no spectacular caves or potholes. Nor are there any great castles or ancient churches. And therein lies its charm. This is a leisurely exploration of a typical Dales landscape, from the ragged clints on the hillside early on, to the banks of the rocky (and sometimes dry) River Skirfare, to the rough grazing of the higher slopes.

Clints and Grikes

At the start of the walk an easy, grassy descent soon brings you to a small area of limestone 'pavement'. Like so much of the Dales landscape, the 'pavements' exist because limestone is soluble.

The slightest cracks or weaknesses in the rock are enlarged by dissolution, and this process is considerably faster when the water has percolated through acidic soil first. The characteristic fissures are known as grikes, and the blocks which are left between them are called clints. The 'pavements' on this walk include some areas where the grikes are still relatively narrow, creating a classic flat 'pavement'. In other areas the grikes are wider and the clints have become more distinct, and you can also see areas where the clints and grikes are still covered by soil.

Dry Beds

You may notice a distinct lack of water, when walking by the Skirfare. It can be lively enough after wet weather but in dry spells the river disappears almost completely, with any remaining water flowing underground. This is due to the permeable nature of the limestone rock. At Foxup Bridge, Cosh Beck and Foxup Beck meet to form the Skirfare, though these streams can also be dry.

After Foxup, the walk climbs away from the valley floor. As the gradient eases is a good time to pause and look back over the last pocket of farmland, directly beyond Foxup on the slope above Cosh Beck. This is a typical patchwork of small fields separated by dry-stone walls and dotted with frequent barns. There are thousands of barns like these in the Yorkshire Dales – nowhere else are they so dense.

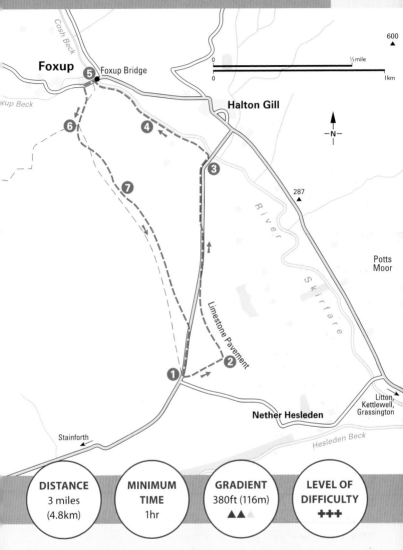

Cosh Beck

600 ▲

Foxup 5 Foxup Bridge

½ mile

1 km

Halton Gill

up Beck

6

4

—N—

7

3

287 ▲

River Skirfare

Potts Moor

Limestone Pavement

2

1

Litton, Kettlewell, Grassington

Nether Hesleden

Stainforth

Hesleden Beck

DISTANCE
3 miles
(4.8km)

MINIMUM TIME
1hr

GRADIENT
380ft (116m)
▲▲▲

LEVEL OF DIFFICULTY
+++

PATHS Riverside paths, moorland tracks and some easy but pathless walking, no stiles **LANDSCAPE** Quintessential mix of green valley, limestone clints and rough moorland **SUGGESTED MAP** OS Explorer OL30 Yorkshire Dales: North & Central **START/FINISH** Grid reference: SD 877749
DOG FRIENDLINESS Be prepared to encounter livestock at all points on this walk
PARKING Wide verges just north of cattle grid on the road from Halton Gill to Stainforth **PUBLIC TOILETS** None on route

WALK 35 DIRECTIONS

❶ From a warning sign just before the cattle grid, turn left and follow a faint green track down the slope, to pass roughly midway between two isolated lengths of stone wall. Continue down, a little more steeply, until the track passes through a broken band of rocks.

❷ Turn left just before the rocks, and walk along the slope keeping them just to your right. They form some small areas of limestone 'pavement', never very extensive. This brings you back to the road. Either walking on the tarmac or on the grass, follow it downhill to the valley floor, where it swings right to Halton Gill Bridge.

❸ Immediately before the bridge, turn left through a little gate (sign to Foxup) and walk near the river to a gate. Continue to another gate and along the field-edge, near the river. Cross two side-streams (plank bridges are available if needed, but they often aren't), then go through another gate to the river bank.

❹ Turn left to a smaller gate, then follow the river to another gate.

There are some attractive cascades hereabouts. Continue along the river bank until you reach a stile and small gate beside the river (the bed is often dry here). Follow the short, narrow path to a lane by Foxup Bridge.

❺ Turn left on the lane; the tarmac soon gives way to gravel. Opposite Foxup farmhouse, with its little stone bridge, turn left at a bridleway sign and follow a track up a small enclosure to a gate. From this the track bears right to a gate near a television aerial.

❻ Don't go through the gate, but follow the track which bends back left, mostly distinguishable as a grassy line between swathes of thistles, to another gate. From this, follow the track parallel to a wall until the wall bends away.

❼ Keep straight ahead on a level course across the moor. The track is never very clear but it is always visible. Go through another gate in a wall that runs down the fellside and continue along the faint track, which keeps more or less level across the moor until it reaches the road. Turn right to complete the circuit.

🍴 EATING AND DRINKING

Just down the dale is the Queen's Arms at Litton, a fine, traditional building with walls up to 2ft (60cm) thick keeping it snug whatever the weather's like outside. It serves good, hearty home-cooked food with local ingredients such as Wharefdale trout, as well as soup and sandwiches for the lighter appetite. It also has its own micro-brewery producing highly regarded real ales.

ATTERMIRE SCAR AND VICTORIA CAVE

Exploring the route to a famous cave,
once host to prehistoric bones.

If Victoria Cave did not exist, this would still be a beautiful walk, and the cave makes it an exceptionally fascinating one. After a steep climb out of Settle, the way stretches more easily across the hillsides, with extensive views of Ribblesdale and Ingleborough. An easy track leads to Attermire Scar and the approach to the cave itself. The path then loops around below the Scar and the jumbled crags of Warrendale Knotts, before descending to rejoin the outward route just above Settle.

Hidden Treasures

The gaping entrance of Victoria Cave is so obvious, you would think it must have been known for centuries, but in fact it was only discovered, by accident, in 1837. This was the year of Queen Victoria's coronation, hence the name. It was also, coincidentally, the same year that Ingleborough Cave (see Walk 39) was revealed. The original entrance is a narrow slit high on the left, and the large entrance you see today is artificial, created by enthusiastic Victorian archaeologists. The green platform just outside the cave is made of spoil dumped from these excavations. Much of the cave was choked with mud, but this proved to be a treasure trove of finds, making it one of the most important caves in the UK.

Discoveries included large numbers of animal remains from the last interglacial period, about 130,000 years ago. Among them are bones of lions, elephants, rhinoceroses and hippopotamuses, all suggesting that the environment was very different then. It's thought that the cave was home to a pack of spotted hyaenas – hyaenas are scavengers, and the other bones were brought in by them. After the last glacial phase, perhaps 10,000 years ago, the cave was occupied by brown bears and subsequently by humans, before being abandoned to the foxes and badgers.

The dangers of rockfall at the cave mouth are self-evident; there are blocks of all sizes scattered around, some of which have fallen recently. Despite this there have been a number of challenging rock climbs made on the walls above, but this has now been banned to protect the archaeological site.

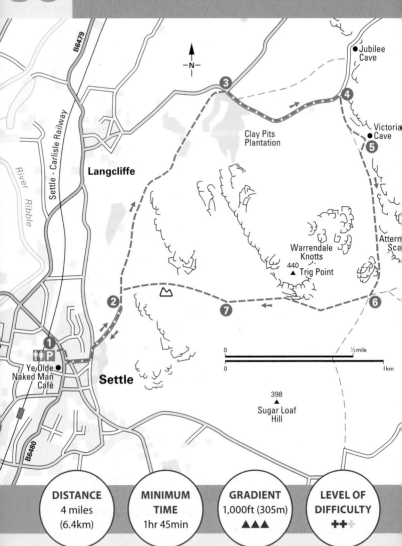

Jubilee
Cave

B6479

Settle - Carlisle Railway

Langcliffe

River Ribble

Clay Pits
Plantation

Victoria
Cave

3

4

5

Warrendale
Knotts
440
▲ Trig Point

Attern
Sca

2

7

6

Ye Olde
Naked Man
Café

Settle

B6480

0   ½ mile
0   1 km

398
▲
Sugar Loaf
Hill

DISTANCE	MINIMUM TIME	GRADIENT	LEVEL OF DIFFICULTY
4 miles (6.4km)	1hr 45min	1,000ft (305m) ▲▲▲	✚✚✚

PATHS Good tracks with some narrower paths; steep, rough climb to the entrance of Victoria Cave; 1 stile **LANDSCAPE** Streets and pastures, green plateau and steep crags **SUGGESTED MAPS** OS Explorer OL2 Yorkshire Dales: South & West or OL41 Forest of Bowland & Ribblesdale **START/FINISH** Grid reference: SD 819637 **DOG FRIENDLINESS** Lead required: beware bikes, horses and sheep **PARKING** Whitefriars car park, Settle **PUBLIC TOILETS** Whitefriars car park, Settle **NOTE** Warning signs on the approach to Victoria Cave advise that it is dangerous to venture inside or even stand at the entrance.

WALK 36 DIRECTIONS

❶ Leave the car park and turn right to the market place. Turn left up the side of the square and continue up Constitution Hill, climbing steeply until the lane bends left and levels out. A few paces on, fork right up a stony track; a Pennine Bridleway signpost is hidden from the actual junction but appears within a few paces. Follow the track uphill until it levels out near a roofless barn.

❷ Continue with a wall on your left, past a signpost and through a gate into another walled section, then continue, still fairly level, with the wall on your left. Go ahead through a gate and along a fainter green track until the ground ahead falls away, then turn right, uphill. Swing back left to a gate just below a small wood. Continue along the track, now clear again, below the wood, through a gate, then rising across a pasture to emerge onto a lane.

❸ Turn right up a track, following the Settle Loop sign. Climb past a wood, then continue across pasture with a wall on your right. Go through a gate, then turn right almost immediately, following a sign to Victoria Cave.

❹ Go through a kissing gate and along a narrow but clear path, with crags up on the left. In about 300yds (274m) the path forks; go up to the left to a green platform below the entrance to Victoria Cave.

❺ Either double back to the lower path and turn left to continue, or take a steeper but shorter path down. Continue along the path, go through a gate, bear right slightly then continue along a level green path. As this descends, becoming stony again, go through a gate half-way down on the right and follow another path down, bearing right below bouldery slopes.

❻ At the bottom turn right along an easier path. Look for a spring among boulders near the junction. Follow the path parallel to a wall, with the crags of Warrendale Knotts up on the right. After a stile the path becomes beautifully green, so good you might think it's mown regularly. Follow the path past the end of a wall, bearing right and then straightening again along another wall.

❼ From a gate the path begins to descend; follow it down the steepening slope, and left through a broken wall to descend to the roofless barn at Point ❷. Retrace the opening stage of the walk back into Settle.

🍴 EATING AND DRINKING

Settle has a good range of pubs, cafés and restaurants, including the long-established Ye Olde Naked Man Café and Bakery which occupies a building dating to 1663. If every table is taken, you can also buy bread (baked on the premises) and sandwiches to take away.

SECRETS OF COCKET MOSS

A rare remnant of undrained wetland is the highlight of this more challenging walk.

Cocket Moss is something special, a fragment of almost primordial landscape. Once, much more of the surrounding lowlands would have looked like this, but human effort over thousands of years has cleared woods and drained wetlands. The central part of Cocket Moss is extremely wet, but fortunately for us there's a causeway across it, which makes it a pleasure to explore – it's not completely primordial, after all.

The rest of the walk may be less remarkable, but it's still full of charm, from the opening stroll along one of the quietest lanes in Yorkshire to the later stages with their delightful jumble of little crags and scattered trees.

What's in a Bog?

Cocket Moss is a rare example of a valley bog, and thereby earns the accolade of Site of Special Scientific Interest (SSSI). The wettest part, crossed by the causeway, is a species-rich mire dominated by bottlesedge, cottongrass and sphagnum mosses. After crossing the causeway, you traverse rough grazing land which is mostly dominated by purple moorgrass *(Molinia caerulea)*. This forms tall tussocks which can make the going a bit slow. The 'purple' in the name refers mainly to the flower head at the tip of the stalk.

Craven Faults

Earlier in the walk, the elevated stretch of lane between two gates has fine views extending to Ingleborough and Pen-y-Ghent. These and other summits rise from extensive plateau-like hills marked with many pale outcrops of limestone. There's no limestone to be seen close at hand, though: the little crags which prettily punctuate the landscape around Cocket Moss are all of millstone grit. You'll pass close to some of these crags later on. The limestone is still there, but buried deep beneath your feet.

This is all part of the influence of the Craven Faults, an ancient series of earth movements which pushed up the rocks to the north and east relative to the ones you're standing on. The faultline runs roughly parallel and just beyond the present-day course of the A65, and is actually crossed on Walk 39.

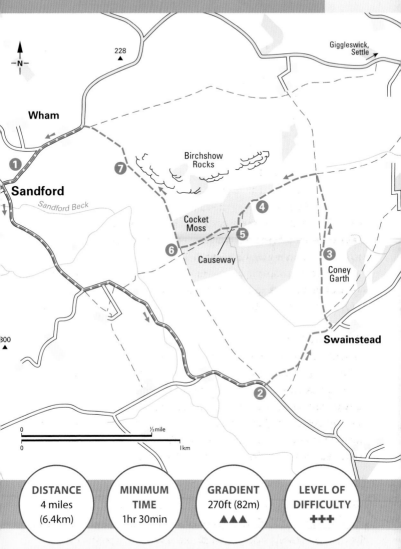

DISTANCE
4 miles
(6.4km)

MINIMUM TIME
1hr 30min

GRADIENT
270ft (82m)
▲▲▲

LEVEL OF DIFFICULTY
+++

PATHS Quiet lane, farm tracks, fields and rough pasture, 3 stiles
LANDSCAPE A mixture of moorland, pasture, open woodland, gritstone crags and mire **SUGGESTED MAP** OS Explorer OL41 Forest of Bowland & Ribblesdale **START/FINISH** Grid reference: SD 774622 **DOG FRIENDLINESS** The safest place for dogs to run free is actually on the almost traffic-free lane **PARKING** Wide verges on Wham Lane between Lower Wham and Sandford **PUBLIC TOILETS** None on route **NOTE** In spring and early summer look out for ground-nesting birds, especially around Cocket Moss; keep dogs strictly on leads at this time

WALK 37 DIRECTIONS

❶ Walk west along the road, with a wall on your left. The lane bends left near a farm then passes through a gate. The next section is pleasantly elevated. Pass through another gate and continue along the winding lane for about 0.75 miles (1.2km) to the wide opening of a stony track on the left.

❷ Turn left down this track and follow it for about 600yds (549m) until it dips down gently before rising again, with a farm on the skyline ahead. In the dip, turn left to cross a stream by the grassed-over remains of a small dam. This is still a water intake (you can see the pump), so take care not to pollute. Go through a gate just beyond (it says 'Bull in Field' in very faded paint). Follow the left-hand wall for around 50yds (46m), then bear slightly right to follow a green track along the flank of a small hill with scattered thorn trees. Continue along the track past dense stands of rushes, and as these thin out turn left to find a stile in a stone wall.

❸ Cross this and turn right immediately, between the wall and a wire fence. When the fence ends bear left across the field to a gate left of a barn. Go straight across the next field to a small gate/stile in a stone wall, below a large ash tree. Cross this, then turn left immediately, following the wall. The ground is quite rough here as it was disturbed by pipeline works in 2008–09. Cross another stile in a wire fence and continue uphill, still following the left-hand wall.

❹ As you start to descend, the wall on your left turns away sharply. Go half left here, roughly level across a slope, then down to a gate in the far corner of the pasture. This gate leads to a grassy causeway which is, very obviously, the only way across a very wet area. This is the heart of Cocket Moss.

❺ Cross the causeway then follow a faint path, just right of a groove, up the slope beyond. From the top of this slope there's no obvious path, but go straight ahead across the rough moor. It's damp, but nowhere near as wet as the area flanking the causeway.

❻ When you reach a faint track, parallel to a wall ahead, turn right. Follow the track to a gate with a tall post, go through and follow the left-hand wall. At the next angle of the wall, below the crag of Birchshow Rocks, bear left; there's a very faint track and you need to keep 99 percent of the boulders to your right. Look for a wire fence on the right, and converge with this as it runs down to a gate.

❼ Go through this gate and straight ahead, below more rocks. Pass the end of a detached section of wall, then bear left to a gate in the far corner, left of some trees. A second gate leads out to the lane; turn left and follow it back to the start.

AROUND RIBBLEHEAD'S MAJESTIC VIADUCT

Discovering the delights of a famous landmark,
a great monument to Victorian engineering.

'Nowhere in the kingdom has nature placed such gigantic obstacles in the way of the railway engineer', observed a newspaper when the Settle–Carlisle railway line was complete. The railway was planned and built by the Midland Railway so it could reach Scotland without trespassing on its rivals' territory of the east or west coast routes. It cost the then enormous sum of £3.5 million and was opened in 1876. The line survived for almost 100 years, until passenger services were withdrawn in 1970. It was said that the viaducts, especially the Ribblehead, were unsafe. There was a public outcry which led to a concerted campaign to keep the line open. Since then there has been a change of heart. Ribblehead is repaired, and the line is one of the most popular – and spectacular – tourist lines in the country.

'A Mighty Work'

It took all of five years to build Ribblehead's huge viaduct. It is 0.25 miles (400m) long, and stands 100ft (30m) high at its maximum; the columns stretch another 25ft (7.6m) into the ground. The stone – more than 30,000 cubic yards (22,950 cubic metres) of it – came from Littledale to the north, and construction progressed from north to south. The area is called Batty Moss, and was inhospitable, to say the least. There is a rumour that the columns are set on bales of wool, as the engineers could not find the bedrock. Romantic as this may sound in a county whose fortunes are largely based on wool, it is untrue; the columns are set in concrete on top of the rock below. There are 24 spans, each 45ft (13.7m) wide. Every sixth column is thicker than its neighbours, so that if one column fell it would take only five others with it, and the whole viaduct would not fall.

Blea Moor and Ancient Farms

The walk takes you past the viaduct to the beginning of Blea Moor, and near perhaps the most exposed signal box in Britain. Beyond it is Blea Moor tunnel, another of the mighty engineering works of the Settle–Carlisle Railway, 2,629yds (2,404m) long and dug by miners working by candlelight.

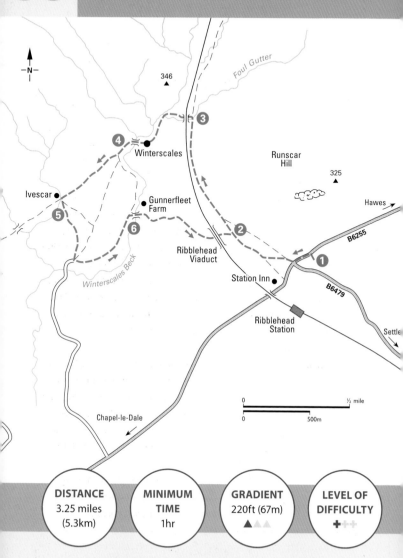

—N—

346 ▲

Foul Gutter

❸

❹
Winterscales ●

Runscar
Hill

325 ▲

Hawes →

B6255

Ivescar ●

❺

● Gunnerfleet
Farm

❻

❷

❶

Ribblehead
Viaduct

B6479

Winterscales Beck

Station Inn ●

Settle →

Ribblehead
Station

Chapel-le-Dale
←

| 0 | | ½ mile |
| 0 | | 500m |

DISTANCE	MINIMUM TIME	GRADIENT	LEVEL OF DIFFICULTY
3.25 miles (5.3km)	1hr	220ft (67m) ▲▲▲	✚✚✚

PATHS Moorland and farm paths and tracks, no stiles
LANDSCAPE Bleak moorland and farmland, dominated by the
Ribblehead Viaduct **SUGGESTED MAP** OS Explorer OL2 Yorkshire Dales:
Southern & Western **START/FINISH** Grid reference: SD 765792
DOG FRIENDLINESS Dogs can be off lead by viaduct, but should be on lead
in farmland **PARKING** Space at junction of B6255 and B6479 near Ribblehead
Viaduct **PUBLIC TOILETS** None on route

WALK 38 DIRECTIONS

❶ From the road junction, with the B6479 at your back, follow green paths towards the viaduct. Turn right on a gravel track and follow it until it turns under the viaduct; continue ahead.

❷ Walk parallel with the railway line above you to your left. Climb steps and continue near the railway and at much the same level. Go through a gate and continue until you reach a railway signal. Go left under a railway arch, following a public bridleway sign.

❸ Follow the track downhill towards the stream, then bear left, roughly parallel to the water, to Winterscales. Go through a gate between the buildings and on to a humpback bridge below a cottage.

> ### ⊘ IN THE AREA
> Take the road – or the train – up to Dent Station. You will pass through the Blea Moor tunnel and then over the Dent Head Viaduct, with its 10 spans, and the same maximum height as Ribblehead.

> ### 🍴 EATING AND DRINKING
> In the summer months an ice-cream van stations itself at the car park, and it's usually there in winter too for hot drinks and snacks. The Station Inn, near the viaduct, offers warmth and comforting home-cooked meals in its bar and dining room.

❹ Follow the lane over a cattle grid, then fork right (almost straight ahead). Keep left at the next fork, pass an isolated cowshed and continue to Ivescar farm. Pass a modern cowshed and then an older barn. Turn left immediately, at the corner of the yard before the farmhouse, down a concrete track.

❺ Follow the track for about 500yds (457m) to a junction and turn sharp left on another tarmac track. Continue for another 500yds (457m) to a farm (Gunnerfleet); turn right over a small bridge just before the farm buildings.

❻ Continue along the track and go under the viaduct, then retrace your steps to the parking place.

> ### 🐾 ON THE WALK
> On a fine summer's day Ribblehead can seem a magical place, with curlews calling and the occasional rumble as a train crosses the viaduct. But it can be one of the bleakest places in the Dales. The average rainfall in the area is 70 inches (178cm), but can often be half as much again. Snow frequently blocks the roads. More difficult for the trains, however, is the wind. Wind speeds of 50 knots are a normal occurrence, and gales can reach a greater speed. Crossing the viaduct becomes a hazardous business. The wife of one signalman stationed at Blea Moor was known for walking across the viaduct to catch the train at Ribblehead Station carrying her baby – one hopes that it was calm weather when she attempted the journey.

Ribblehead Viaduct crossing the moor

INGLEBOROUGH CAVE AND TROW GILL

Geography comes to life here, with faults,
caves and gorges all on show.

The walk begins by following a nature trail through the Ingleborough Estate.
This area owes much of its present lush appearance to the work of Reginald
Farrer (1880–1920). Farrer became an eminent botanist and plant-collector,
travelling extensively in Asia. He had a massive influence on the development
of rockgardening but it's recorded that he encouraged plants to colonise rock
faces by firing seeds from a shotgun!

Beneath the Surface

Beyond the nature trail you soon reach Ingleborough Cave. Its calcite flows,
stalactites and stalagmites weren't discovered until 1837, when a natural dam
which had blocked access was washed away in a flood. It was soon turned
into a showcave, and has been one ever since.

The stream which formed Ingleborough Cave has altered its underground
course and now appears close by at Beck Head. This is the same stream which
disappears into the ground at Gaping Gill, possibly the most famous pothole
in Britain. This fact was established long ago through dyetests, but the actual
connection between the two ends of the system was not completed until
1983 and involved serious cavediving.

Gaping Gill is an aptly named hole in the moor about 0.75 miles (1.2km)
beyond the head of Trow Gill. Its main shaft is 328ft (100m) deep, and the
waterfall is the highest unbroken fall in Britain. It is normally inaccessible
to non-cavers, but on two occasions each year a winch is set up to allow
members of the public to descend into the chamber. Bradford Pothole Club
runs a winch meet at the late May bank holiday, and Craven Pothole Club at
the August bank holiday weekend.

Record Breaker

The shaft was the deepest known until the discovery of Titan, in Derbyshire,
in 2006. The cavern at the bottom of Gaping Gill, known as the Main Chamber,
is the largest known cavern in Britain: 475ft (145m) long, 82ft (25m) wide and
115ft (35m) high.

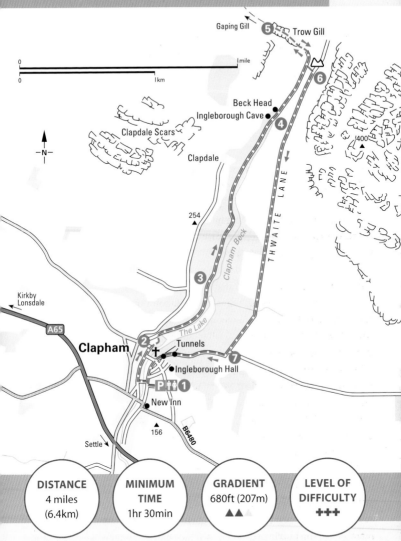

DISTANCE	MINIMUM TIME	GRADIENT	LEVEL OF DIFFICULTY
4 miles (6.4km)	1hr 30min	680ft (207m) ▲▲▲	+++

PATHS Generally easy, surfaced tracks, rougher near Trow Gill, and one short, steep, rough linking section; 2 stiles **LANDSCAPE** Lush cultivated grounds, a wilder valley and a descent through wide pastures **SUGGESTED MAP** OS Explorer OL2 Yorkshire Dales: South & West **START/FINISH** Grid reference: SD 745692 **DOG FRIENDLINESS** Mostly enclosed tracks, but beware mountain bikes in the later stages **PARKING** Clapham (pay-and-display) **PUBLIC TOILETS** At car park, Clapham **NOTE** A small fee (currently 50p) is charged for access to the Ingleborough Estate Nature Trail. Take a torch with you for the tunnel section

WALK 39 DIRECTIONS

❶ Turn right out of the car park, then very soon turn left to cross a narrow bridge. Turn right, parallel to the stream, and walk up the road. Pass a viewpoint for the falls on the right, and then arrive at the entrance to the Ingleborough Estate Nature Trail. Pay the small fee at the machine and collect a leaflet for more information.

❷ Walk up the obvious track to arrive beside a small lake. Continue along the level track beside the water and then, near the end of the lake, begin to climb gently again, crossing a small bridge at post 10 of the Nature Trail.

> ### 🍴 EATING AND DRINKING
> Clapham's New Inn is popular with cavers. There's plenty to like, from a fine panelled interior to a selection of real ales, mostly from nearby breweries such as Moorhouse's and Copper Dragon, and a menu that's focused on fresh local ingredients. There are also several cafés in the village.

❸ Continue past a large grotto on the left. Exit the woodland into more open surroundings and continue straight ahead to arrive at Ingleborough Cave with its impressive entrance.

❹ The main track continues over a small bridge. Look left here to see the stream emerging from another cave entrance, known as Beck Head. Continue along the track, now rougher.

> ### 🌀 IN THE AREA
> Take time out from the walk to visit Ingleborough Cave (open daily for most of the year, but by appointment only from November to mid-February). Tours start on the hour, take about 50 minutes. At weekends in December the Cave also becomes a rather special Santa's Grotto.

Where it bends left, note a stile on the right, but for now continue up and through a gate into the narrowing gorge of Trow Gill.

❺ Turn around and backtrack to the bend in the track. This time cross the stile and go up a steep, rough path, slightly to the right. Continue more easily to another stile in the next wall.

❻ Cross the stile to a track (Thwaite Lane) and turn right. Follow the track steadily downhill. The easy walking allows leisure to look out over the very different scenery of the Forest of Bowland. Continue through a steeper dip and up a slight rise to reach a junction.

❼ Turn right. The track descends through two tunnels. These are quite dark (especially the first one) and some people will feel happier with a torch. Emerge just above the parish church, and skirt round the churchyard to meet a lane. Turn left and it soon leads back to the car park.

ABOVE AND BELOW GROUND AT KINGSDALE

Take the chance to gaze at several spectacular potholes, and even venture underground yourself.

This is a rare chance for ordinary walkers to taste the esoteric delights of caving, in reasonable comfort and safety. However, there are also some deep and manifestly hazardous holes on this walk. None of them are fenced, and they should be approached with caution. The edges may be sloping or crumbly. Dogs should be on leads, and children kept under close supervision.

But don't let this put you off. These dangers are obvious and all that's needed is a modicum of common sense. There's also a simple passage, just below the surface, with a safe entry and exit. In fact, if you take the first exit, you won't even need a torch. Tall people will need to stoop a bit, but that's about all.

Going Underground

Rowten Pot and Jingling Pot are deep and obvious holes, for cavers only, but a smaller passage at Point ❸ is inviting to intrepid walkers. Scramble down beside the stream and look into the main passage where the stream runs into the darkness. Turn right and you'll see another passage, with a smaller stream emerging from it (sometimes dry). Enter this (tall people will need to stoop), and follow for about 30ft (9m) to another opening, where you can scramble out. There's enough light filtering in for this to be possible without a torch. If you have torches you can also continue about another 60ft (18m) to a final exit.

There's another short passage indicated at Jingling Cave. This is also safe, but it's low – adults will have to crouch, if not crawl – and it's usually wet. Of course low, wet passages are a common experience for cavers, and at least this one is light. Do not enter any other passages.

Nearby Jingling Pot is the most alarming and potentially dangerous hole on this walk. The name almost certainly derives from the sound of water falling on stones in the depths: the bottom is 150ft (46m) down. All of these caves and potholes are part of the West Kinsgdale System, itself part of the Three Counties System, in which cavers have now charted over 70 miles (113km) of passages.

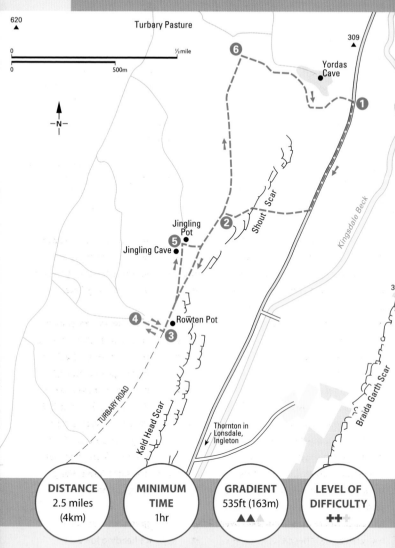

DISTANCE
2.5 miles
(4km)

MINIMUM TIME
1hr

GRADIENT
535ft (163m)
▲▲▲

LEVEL OF DIFFICULTY
✛✛✛

PATHS Easy tracks and generally clear; caving optional
LANDSCAPE A high hanging valley and open fellsides
SUGGESTED MAP OS Explorer OL2 Yorkshire Dales: South & West
START/FINISH Grid reference: SD 706790
DOG FRIENDLINESS Keep on lead near caves/potholes, as well as near livestock
PARKING Roadside spaces below wooded enclosure (Yordas Cave) 547yds (500m)
south of Kingsdale Head **PUBLIC TOILETS** None on route **NOTE** Take a torch for
further exploration at Point ❷

WALK 40 DIRECTIONS

❶ Walk south down the road (towards Ingleton) for about 500yds (457m) to a gate on the right. Directly above is a crag (Shout Scar) with some trees growing from it. Walk up a green track aiming left of this crag, to an obvious gap through the band of rocks. Above this bear left to meet a wall where it crosses another low band of rocks. Follow the wall up to meet a clear track.

❷ Turn left through a gate and follow the track beside a wall to some sheep pens. Go through two gates close together. Just beyond, a few strides away to the left, is an obvious large hole in the ground, Rowten Pot.

❸ Near the far end of the Pot a sort of natural bridge separates the main opening from a smaller but even deeper hole. Turn your back on the 'bridge' and walk straight back towards the track. Just beside it is a slit in the ground where an underground stream can be seen. Go straight across the track to a narrow path and follow this across the moor for about 90yds (82m) to a place where the stream spills over rocky steps and disappears into the ground. You can venture underground here (see Background).

❹ Return to the main track and turn left. Retrace your steps through the two gates, and continue for 150yds (137m) until a fainter track bears away left across the moor. Follow this

> ### 🍺 EATING AND DRINKING
> Head west and the first pub you come to is the Marton Arms, in the tiny village of Thornton-in-Lonsdale. It has a long-standing reputation for the range and quality of its beer, with 16 handpumps on the bar. There's also an astonishing 280 malt whiskies to choose from. An appropriately pubby menu is served in hearty portions.

towards a substantial, isolated rowan tree. On the left as you approach the tree is another short passage with two entrances, part of Jingling Cave.

❺ The tree grows from a deep shaft, Jingling Pot. From here return straight across the moor to the main track and turn left. From the gate at Point ❷, instead of retracing your steps down the hill, continue along the track. This soon bears left and climbs gently to reach another gate. Continue along the now rougher track, beside a wall, to a gate on the right. Several large boulders restrict its opening.

❻ Follow a green track downhill from this gate heading towards some trees. Just above them the track swings right and down, then back left to a gate onto the road near the parking places. Before heading home, however, it's worth turning uphill just above the gate, into the trees, to find the entrance to Yordas Cave.

Walking in Safety

All these walks are suitable for any reasonably fit person, but less experienced walkers should try the easier walks first. Route finding is usually straightforward, but you will find that an Ordnance Survey map is a useful addition to the route maps and descriptions.

RISKS

Although each walk here has been researched with a view to minimising the risks to the walkers who follow its route, no walk in the countryside can be considered to be completely free from risk. Walking in the outdoors will always require a degree of common sense and judgement to ensure that it is as safe as possible.

- Be particularly careful on cliff paths and in upland terrain, where the consequences of a slip can be very serious.
- Remember to check tidal conditions before walking on the seashore.
- Some sections of route are by, or cross, busy roads. Take care and remember traffic is a danger even on minor country lanes.
- Be careful around farmyard machinery and livestock, especially if you have children with you.
- Be aware of the consequences of changes in the weather and check the forecast before you set out. Carry spare clothing and a torch if you are walking in the winter months. Remember the weather can change very quickly at any time of the year, and in moorland and heathland areas, mist and fog can make route finding much harder. Don't set out in these conditions unless you are confident of your navigation skills in poor visibility. In summer remember to take account of the heat and sun; wear a hat and carry spare water.

On walks away from centres of population you should carry a whistle and survival bag. If you do have an accident requiring the emergency services, make a note of your position as accurately as possible and dial 999.

COUNTRYSIDE CODE

- Be safe, plan ahead and follow any signs.
- Leave gates and property as you find them.
- Protect plants and animals and take your litter home.
- Keep dogs under close control.
- Consider other people.

For more information on the Countryside Code visit:
www.naturalengland.org.uk/ourwork/enjoying/countrysidecode